Empirical Generalizations about Marketing Impact

What we have learned from academic research

Empirical Generalizations about Marketing Impact

What we have learned from academic research

DOMINIQUE M. HANSSENS, Editor

MARKETING SCIENCE INSTITUTE
Cambridge, Massachusetts

Copyright 2009 Marketing Science Institute
Published by Marketing Science Institute, 1000 Massachusetts Ave.,
Cambridge, MA 02138
Printed in the United States of America
ISBN-10 0-9823877-0-9
ISBN-13 978-0-9823877-0-2

Cover by Joyce C. Weston
Book design by Laughlin Winkler

Contents

Foreword

For a number of years, a top MSI research priority has been to better understand the impact of marketing spending on performance. CMOs and other senior marketing managers need not only to improve the measurement and allocation of marketing activities, but also to justify marketing spending to others such as CFOs and CEOs. That this continues to be a high priority for MSI member companies is reflected by the fact that it is the number one research priority for the period 2008–10.

In this book, the eighth in our Relevant Knowledge Series, Dominique Hanssens of UCLA's Anderson School provides an invaluable service to the practitioner and academic communities by surveying academic research to determine what we know about the impact of marketing activities on product and firm performance. He is in a unique position to produce this book, both from his tenure as MSI Executive Director (2005–07) and from his vast research experience on estimating the impact of marketing spending at both the product and firm levels.

For the collection, Hanssens has surveyed academic experts across 16 different topic areas to provide general findings that have emerged over many years of academic research. Each contribution describes the empirical generalization, the evidence supporting the generalization, and the managerial implications. Of additional value are reference citations so that interested readers can obtain more details about the study and its findings. Taken together, the findings in *Empirical Generalizations about Marketing Impact* provide an outstanding summary of what we know about how marketing spending affects a variety of performance metrics.

This book is a "must read" for any practitioner or academic interested in what empirical research has to say about the impact of marketing on products and the firm. We are very pleased to add it to MSI's Relevant Knowledge Series, and we thank Dominique Hanssens for his outstanding contribution.

Russell S. Winer
New York University
MSI Executive Director 2007–09

Introduction

There is a natural tendency of managers to think of markets for which they are responsible as unique; this tends to limit search for information to perfect or near-perfect matches with the problem at hand, and has so far robbed many managers of a strategically important research tool.

—John U. Farley, Donald R. Lehmann, and Alan Sawyer (1995), "Empirical Marketing Generalization Using Meta-Analysis," *Marketing Science* 14 (30) (Part 2 of 2), G45

The wisdom of this observation rings through as clearly in this decade as when it was written. Yet continued research on marketing impact, published in the leading journals, has resulted in the discovery of many patterns that are remarkably replicable, even if the perfect matching conditions don't exist.

The purpose of this volume is to bring these results together in a format and a language that are readily accessible to marketing executives and researchers. I started the process by consulting the *Marketing Science* "Special Issue on Empirical Generalizations in Marketing" published in summer 1995, as well as the published articles in the major scientific marketing journals since then. That review allowed me to identify over 60 authors with proven expertise in one or more marketing areas that are amenable to empirical generalizations.

In summer 2008 I invited these academics to contribute one or more empirical generalizations to a volume in the MSI Relevant Knowledge Series, using a simple, standardized one-page format. In terms of content, I asked for generalizations that deal with marketing impact, broadly defined, and I encouraged authors to quantify their statements to the extent possible. In terms of scientific rigor, I asked for results from proper meta-analyses (that is, studies of studies conducted independently by several authors), and from single studies that encompass a large number of replications (for example, across several brands, categories, regional markets, etc.). In all cases the limitations of the generalization are clearly identified; for example, it may have been tested only in business-to-consumer settings. I also requested careful source documentation, so the interested reader may have ready access to the detailed reports, as well as a statement of managerial relevance of the generalization.

The response to my request was very encouraging, with nearly all colleagues volunteering to participate, in many cases with several generalizations. A few academics felt that, in their area of expertise, no empirical generalizations exist at this juncture. In the conclusion, I identify these cases, which present "knowledge gaps" in our discipline and therefore offer important areas for future research.

Even though the generalizations or benchmarks in this volume are taken from the leading scientific journals, they are expressed as much as possible in the language of marketing decision makers. In some cases, technical terms are necessary, especially as they relate to statistical measures. For those who are less familiar with such technical terms, I have provided a glossary of definitions in the following pages.

The reader may find some of these empirical generalizations (EGs in short) confirm his or her prior beliefs, some will be surprising, and others may be totally new. In interpreting these findings, bear in mind that marketing is a social science, not a physical science in which mathematical laws such as $E = mc^2$ may be derived. The authors of the generalizations have been careful to state the boundaries of their findings, and as research in marketing progresses, these boundaries will become better and better defined. On occasion I have allowed for some overlap among the generalizations across authors, though each generalization always makes a unique contribution.

I am grateful to the Marketing Science Institute for their willingness to disseminate this collection of impact benchmarks as part of MSI's Relevant Knowledge Series. Above all, I thank the numerous colleagues from around the world who were generous with their time and expertise as they contributed one or more generalizations.

Dominique M. Hanssens

Glossary

The following metrics and statistics are frequently used in the empirical generalizations. They are generally obtained either by statistical analysis of historical data or by controlled experiments.

Coefficient of variation: the standard deviation of a variable, divided by its mean.

Correlation (r): a measure of linear association between two variables X and Y, ranging between -1 and $+1$. The higher the correlation in absolute value, the more tightly the two variables co-move with each other. Correlation measures linear association, but does not establish the direction of causality between X and Y.

Diffusion of innovation: the coefficient of innovation (p) is the fraction of first purchasers who are innovators in the sense that they are not influenced by other buyers. For example, $p = .02$ means that 2 percent of the eventual adopters of a new durable product or service are innovators (and therefore 2 percent of total adoption sales are realized in the first period).

Diffusion of innovation: the coefficient of imitation (q) reflects the speed of imitation among first purchasers of a new durable product or service. The higher the value q, the stronger the influence of previous buyers on future buyers, through word-of-mouth and network effects. For a new product to be commercially successful, $q > p$, but if q is only marginally greater than p, diffusion will be slow and protracted.

Elasticity: a measure of the relative impact of a change in a variable X on another variable Y, defined as percent change in Y divided by percent change in X. For example, an advertising-to-sales elasticity of .08 means that, all else equal, an increase in advertising spending of 10% results in a sales increase of .8%. Elasticity implies a causal direction.

Eta (η), or the correlation ratio between X and Y, is the square root of the proportion of the variance of Y accounted for by X.

Gini coefficient: a measure of income inequality in a country, scaled between 0 and 1. The lower the Gini coefficient, the more equal the income distribution, and vice versa.

Hofstede culture assessment: a five-dimensional scale that measures a country or culture's orientation toward individualism/collectivism, high/low power distance, masculinity/femininity, uncertainty avoidance, and long- versus short-term orientation.

Empirical Generalizations about Marketing Impact

What we have learned from academic research

1

Market Orientation and Marketing Capabilities

Marketing Capabilities

The linear relationship between marketing capability and firm performance is positive ($r = .35$) and stronger than those for R&D ($r = .28$) or operations ($r = .21$) capabilities.

Evidence base	114 studies reporting 786 effect sizes
Managerial implications	Increase in marketing capability is associated with stronger improvement in firm performance than increases in operations capability and R&D capability.
Contributors	Alexander Krasnikov, George Washington University, and Satish Jayachandran, University of South Carolina
Reference	Krasnikov, Alexander, and Satish Jayachandran (2008), "The Relative Impact of Marketing, Research-and-Development, and Operations Capabilities on Firm Performance," *Journal of Marketing* 72 (4), 1–11

Service Transition Strategy

Service transition strategies, i.e., moving from a product- to a service-centric business, add to shareholder value. However, the positive impact of service transition strategies only starts to affect shareholder value when the firm reaches a critical mass of services sales of 20–30%, at which point they have an increasingly positive effect.

Evidence base	477 publicly traded U.S. manufacturing firms during 1990–2005
Managerial implications	Service transition strategies may fail to generate shareholder value if the push into services is half-hearted. Companies should recognize that service transition strategies typically require building a critical mass in sales of services-to-products ratio in the product/service portfolio, estimated to be 20–30%, before they can expect positive effects on shareholder value.
Contributor	Jan-Benedict E.M. Steenkamp, University of North Carolina
Reference	Fang, Eric, Robert W. Palmatier, and Jan-Benedict E.M. Steenkamp (2008), "Effect of Service Transition Strategies on Firm Value." *Journal of Marketing* 72 (5), 1–14

Impact of Market Orientation

Market orientation (i.e., the organizational activities related to the generation and dissemination of and responsiveness to market intelligence, as well as the organizational norms and values that encourage behaviors consistent with market orientation) has a positive effect on organizational performance ($r = .32$), as measured by profits, sales, and market share. The market orientation–performance correlation is higher in manufacturing businesses ($r = .37$), compared to service businesses ($r = .26$). The association is stronger in countries that are low rather than high on power distance (i.e., how society deals with the fact that people are unequal in physical and intellectual capabilities) ($r = .33$ versus $r = .27$) and uncertainty avoidance (i.e., the extent to which a culture socializes its members into accepting ambiguous situations and tolerating uncertainty) ($r = .34$ versus $r = .27$).

Evidence base	Meta-analysis of 114 prior studies
Managerial implications	Market orientation provides a competitive advantage that leads to superior organizational performance. Even though the implementation of market orientation demands resources, it generates profits over and above the costs involved in its implementation, while concurrently growing revenues. This impact is greater in manufacturing businesses than in service industries. The implementation of market orientation processes should be adapted to local cultural sensitivities.
Contributors	William O. Bearden, University of South Carolina, Satish Jayachandran, University of South Carolina, and Ahmet H. Kirca, Michigan State University
Reference	Kirca, Ahmet H., Satish Jayachandran, and William O. Bearden (2005), "Market Orientation: A Meta-Analytic Review and Assessment of Its Antecedents and Impact on Performance," *Journal of Marketing* 69 (2), 24–41

Drivers of Market Orientation

While interdepartmental connectedness (i.e., the degree of formal and informal contact among employees across departments) has the strongest impact on market orientation ($r = .56$), top management emphasis (i.e., top management reinforcement of the importance of a market orientation) ($r = .44$) and market-based reward systems (i.e., reliance on market-based factors, such as customer satisfaction, for evaluating and rewarding managers and employees in organizations) ($r = .41$) also positively affect a firm's market orientation.

Evidence base	Meta-analysis of 114 prior studies
Managerial implications	By ensuring top management emphasis, interdepartmental connectedness, and customer-satisfaction-based reward systems, market orientation can be effectively implemented in organizations.
Contributors	William O. Bearden, University of South Carolina, Satish Jayachandran, University of South Carolina, and Ahmet H. Kirca, Michigan State University
Reference	Kirca, Ahmet H., Satish Jayachandran, and William O. Bearden (2005), "Market Orientation: A Meta-Analytic Review and Assessment of Its Antecedents and Impact on Performance." *Journal of Marketing* 69 (2), 24–41

2

Effects of Economic Cycles

Consumer Durables and Business Cycles

Consumer durables are more sensitive to business-cycle fluctuations than most other sectors in the economy. The average cyclical volatility (measured as the standard deviation of the cyclical component in the series, which is obtained after filtering out the very short- and long-run fluctuations in the series) is more than four times that of GNP's cyclical component, and the average co-movement elasticity (expressing the extent to which cyclical fluctuations in the economy are translated into cyclical fluctuations in the series of interest) is larger than two.

Evidence base	Diffusion of 24 consumer durables in the U.S. over multiple decades
Managerial implications	Managers should explicitly consider the cyclical variation in the sales of durable products, especially since the extent of this sensitivity can be moderated through the products' pricing strategy. This sensitivity is asymmetric across expansions and contractions, as durable sales fall more quickly during contractions than they recover during economic expansions.
Contributors	Barbara Deleersnyder, Tilburg University, and Marnik G. Dekimpe, Tilburg University and Catholic University of Leuven
Reference	Deleersnyder, Barbara, Marnik G. Dekimpe, Miklos Sarvary, and Philip M. Parker (2004), "Weathering Tight Economic Times: The Sales Evolution of Consumer Durables Over the Business Cycle." *Quantitative Marketing and Economics* 2 (4), 347–83

Advertising and Business Cycles

Advertising is more sensitive to business-cycle fluctuations than the economy as a whole, with an average co-movement elasticity of 1.4. Hence, a 1% increase (reduction) in the cyclical component of GDP (obtained after filtering out both the very short-run fluctuations and the long-run trend) translates, on average, into a 1.4% increase (reduction) in the cyclical component of the demand for advertising. The extent of this sensitivity varies systematically across countries depending on cultural and socio-economic factors. When companies tie their advertising spending too tightly to business cycles, managerial and social losses are incurred. These losses extend far beyond the recession period, and are reflected in (1) a lower long-term growth of the advertising industry, (2) a higher private label share, and (3) lower stock prices.

Evidence base	Advertising spending in 37 countries, across all continents, covering up to 25 years and four media: magazines, newspapers, radio, and television
Managerial implications	Countries where advertising spending behaves more cyclically exhibit slower growth of the advertising industry and higher private label growth. Stock-price performance is lower for companies that exhibit stronger pro-cyclical spending patterns. Systematic differences in cyclical sensitivity across both countries and media offer risk-diversification opportunities.
Contributors	Barbara Deleersnyder, Tilburg University, Marnik G. Dekimpe, Tilburg University and Catholic University of Leuven, and Jan-Benedict E.M. Steenkamp, University of North Carolina at Chapel Hill
Reference	Deleersnyder, Barbara, Marnik G. Dekimpe, Jan-Benedict E.M. Steenkamp, and Peter S.H. Leeflang (2009), "The Role of National Culture in Advertising's Sensitivity to Business Cycles: An Investigation across Continents." *Journal of Marketing Research*, forthcoming

Private Label Share and Business Cycles

Private label share behaves counter-cyclically. A 1% reduction in the cyclical component of GDP per capita translates into an increase of .96% in the cyclical component of private label share, and vice versa. Moreover, consumers switch more extensively to store brands during recessions than they switch back to national brands in a subsequent recovery. Finally, a substantial fraction keeps on buying the private labels even when bad economic times are long over. Specifically, when GDP per capita decreases 1% compared to the peak just before the contraction, a long-run upward lift in private label growth of 1.22% occurs.

Evidence base	Evolution of private label share over multiple decades in the U.S., Germany, Belgium, and the U.K.
Managerial implications	Many consumers switch to private labels during an economic contraction, but not all of them switch back to national brands when the economy improves again. Hence, economic recessions contribute to the prolonged upward evolution in private label share. While business-cycle fluctuations are beyond the control of individual managers, they may mitigate the impact of an economic downturn on their brands' position by engaging in "proactive marketing," i.e., adopt a strategy in which they invest aggressively in marketing activities during the recession. Such a strategy is not often observed in the market.
Contributors	Barbara Deleersnyder, Tilburg University, Marnik G. Dekimpe, Tilburg University and Catholic University of Leuven, and Jan-Benedict E.M. Steenkamp, University of North Carolina at Chapel Hill
Reference	Lamey, Lien, Barbara Deleersnyder, Marnik G. Dekimpe, and Jan-Benedict E.M. Steenkamp (2007), "How Business Cycles Contribute to Private-Label Success: Evidence from the United States and Europe." *Journal of Marketing* 71 (1), 1–15

3

Customer Satisfaction

Customer Satisfaction and Business Performance

Customer satisfaction with firms, as obtained by the American Customer Satisfaction Index, is a significant predictor (explaining 5–9% of the variance) of these firms' future accounting cash flow levels and variability, sales growth, and gross margins, as well as their financial market Tobin's Q (firm's market value to the replacement cost of its assets) and total shareholder returns.

Evidence base	A number of different analyses of over 200 firms in the American Customer Satisfaction Index from 1994 to 2003
Managerial implications	Achieving high levels of customer satisfaction has significant financial pay-offs in terms of accounting-based measures of financial performance and financial-market-based measures of shareholder value.
Contributors	Neil A. Morgan, Indiana University, and Lopo Rego, University of Iowa
References	Gruca, Thomas S., and Lopo L. Rego (2005), "Customer Satisfaction, Cash Flow, and Shareholder Value." *Journal of Marketing* 69 (3), 115–30
	Morgan, Neil A., and Lopo L. Rego (2006), "The Value of Different Customer Satisfaction and Loyalty Metrics in Predicting Business Performance." *Marketing Science* 25 (5), 426–39

Customer Satisfaction and Market Share

The average correlation between customer satisfaction and market share is −.18. It is more negative for product-focused firms and less negative for service-focused firms and those selling less frequently purchased products and services.

Evidence base	Analysis of 200+ firms in the American Customer Satisfaction Index from 1994 to 2003
Managerial implications	The positive impact of raising customer satisfaction on demand is usually outweighed by the difficulty of meeting the heterogeneity of preferences among a wider customer base. Using differentiated offerings for different segments in the customer base or mass customization approaches may enable firms to overcome these difficulties.
Contributors	Neil A. Morgan, Indiana University, Lopo Rego, University of Iowa, and Claes Fornell, University of Michigan
References	Fornell, Claes (1995), "The Quality of Economic Output: Empirical Generalizations About Its Distribution and Relationship to Market Share." *Marketing Science* 14 (3) (Part 2 of 2), G203–11
	Rego, Lopo L., Neil A. Morgan, and Claes Fornell (2008), "The Customer Satisfaction-Market Share Relationship: Empirical Generalizations and Marketing Implications." Ann Arbor, Mich.: University of Michigan, American Customer Satisfaction Index Center, Working Paper

Service Failure and Customer Compensation

Compensation for a service failure (a substandard service performance as a result of either the service provider or an external factor) enhances repurchase intentions only when the company is responsible for the failure and the failure occurs frequently (weighted $\eta = .36$). If the failure occurs infrequently or the company is not responsible, compensation does not affect repurchase intentions.

Evidence base	Meta-analysis of four studies. Additionally, file drawer statistics indicate that it would require 45 null studies to reduce the significance level to .05 level.
Managerial implications	Companies must maintain well-developed service recovery strategies (i.e., compensation, apology) to manage consumers' post-failure evaluations, but they also need to know exactly when to use them. When the failure is an infrequent occurrence or the company is not responsible for it, consumers do not expect to be compensated. Thus, compensation may have minimum to no impact and be a wasted resource.
Contributors	Dhruv Grewal, Babson College, Anne Roggeveen, Babson College, and Michael Tsiros, University of Miami and ALBA Graduate Business School
Reference	Grewal, Dhruv, Anne L. Roggeveen, and Michael Tsiros (2008), "The Effect of Compensation on Repurchase Intentions in Service Recovery," *Journal of Retailing* 84 (4), 424–34

Buyer–Supplier Relationships

Effect size refers to the strength of the relationship between two factors or variables. Satisfaction with buyer–supplier business-to-business (B-to-B) relationships is enhanced by trust (effect size = .64), commitment (effect size = .41), and dependence (effect size = .34). Conflict in buyer–supplier B-to-B relationships is directly reduced by trust (effect size = –.69) and commitment (effect size = –.57). Trust in buyer–supplier B-to-B relationships is enhanced by cooperation (effect size = .55) and dedicated investments made for the particular relationships that have limited value outside the relationship, i.e., transaction-specific investments (effect size = .26). Commitment in buyer–supplier B-to-B relationships is enhanced by trust (effect size = .59), dependence (effect size = .31), and transaction-specific investments (effect size = .35) and reduced by environmental uncertainty (effect size = –.16).

Evidence base	Meta-analysis of 114 measurement error corrected and sample size weighted correlations from 102 studies consisting of 26,828 B-to-B relationships
Managerial implications	Satisfaction and continuity intentions in B-to-B buyer–supplier relationships are driven primarily by relational factors. Environmental factors play a very minor role.
Contributors	Kapil Tuli, Singapore Management University, and Sundar Bharadwaj, Emory University
Reference	Tuli, Kapil, and Sundar Bharadwaj (2007), "Theory and Methodological Artifacts in Customer-Firm Relationships: A Meta-Analytical Review and Integrative Extension." Atlanta, Ga.: Emory University, Goizueta Business School, Working Paper

Relationship Marketing

The average correlation coefficient (sample-weighted reliability adjusted) between the strength of a customer's relationship with a seller (i.e., trust and commitment) and (1) customer loyalty is .52, and (2) objective business performance is .35.

Evidence base	Meta-analysis of approximately 20,000 seller–customer relationships
Managerial implications	The strength of the seller–customer relationship has a strong impact on customer loyalty and performance.
Contributor	Robert W. Palmatier, University of Washington
Reference	Palmatier, Robert W., Rajiv P. Dant, Dhruv Grewal, and Kenneth R. Evans (2006), "Factors Influencing the Effectiveness of Relationship Marketing: A Meta-Analysis." *Journal of Marketing* 70 (4), 136–53

Online Trust

Consumer trust in online firms mediates the effects of site design on behavioral intent (intent to try or repeat purchase). Navigation/ presentation, advice, and brand are as important as privacy and security in establishing trust, but importance varies by product category. Navigation is more important on information-intensive sites (e. g., sports, portals). Brand is more important in high-involvement categories (e.g., autos and finance) and privacy is most important on information-risk sites (e.g., travel).

Evidence base	25 sites across eight categories and 6,831 consumer interviews
Managerial implications	Consumer trust in an Internet site is important to achieving sales. Trust is dependent not only on privacy and security, but also on good navigation, impartial advice, and brand strength. Relative importance depends on site category. Site design should receive careful design and testing efforts.
Contributor	Glen L. Urban, MIT
Reference	Yakov, Bart, Venkatesh Shankar, Fareena Sultan, and Glen L. Urban (2005), "Are the Drivers and Role of Online Trust the Same for All Web Sites and Consumers? A Large-Scale Exploratory Empirical Study." *Journal of Marketing* 69 (4), 133–52

4

Objective and Perceived Quality

Customers' Objective and Subjective Knowledge

The average correlation between what consumers know (objective knowledge) and what they think they know (subjective/perceived knowledge) about various products, services, and other marketing contexts is .37.

Evidence base	Meta-analysis of 51 prior studies
Managerial implications	Consumers' beliefs regarding their level of knowledge of various products, services, and other marketing contexts are related to the amount of their actual knowledge, but not strongly. Combining the meta-analysis results with Ailawadi, Dant, and Grewal's (2004) research, self-report data are likely to demonstrate modest correspondence with objective data. For example, a firm's self-reported innovation capability is probably positively but only modestly related to its actual innovation capability.
Contributors	William O. Bearden, University of South Carolina, Jay P. Carlson, Union Graduate College, David M. Hardesty, University of Kentucky, and Leslie H. Vincent, University of Kentucky
References	Ailawadi, Kusum L., Rajiv P. Dant, and Dhruv Grewal (2004), "The Difference Between Perceptual and Objective Performance Measures: An Empirical Analysis." Cambridge, Mass.: Marketing Science Institute, Report No. 04–103
	Carlson, Jay P., Leslie H. Vincent, David M. Hardesty, and William O. Bearden (2009), "Objective and Subjective Knowledge Relationships: A Quantitative Analysis of Consumer Research Findings." *Journal of Consumer Research* 35 (5), 864–76

Objective and Perceived Quality

A change in objective quality is not fully reflected in customer perceptions of quality until after about six years on average. Across categories, the range is three to nine years. In the first year, only about 20% of the total effect is realized. These effects are larger and occur more quickly for decreases in quality relative to increases in quality. High-reputation brands are rewarded three years faster for quality increases and punished one year more slowly for quality decreases relative to lower-reputation brands.

Evidence base	241 products in 46 product categories over 12 years
Managerial implications	A firm's investments in product quality will pay off over the long term. High-reputation brands enjoy an advantage when competing on quality because consumers update their favorable perceptions more quickly. Firms should track both objective quality and perceived quality, along with its associated lags, in order to develop the appropriate quality strategy.
Contributors	Debanjan Mitra, University of Florida, and Peter N. Golder, New York University
Reference	Mitra, Debanjan, and Peter N. Golder (2006), "How Does Objective Quality Affect Perceived Quality? Short-Term Effects, Long-Term Effects, and Asymmetries." *Marketing Science* 25 (3), 230–47

5

Market Share

Performance Evolution

Sales levels tend to evolve over multiple years (68% of cases); this is especially true for category or industry sales (92% of cases). However, market share tends to be stable over time (78% of cases).

Evidence base	Meta-analysis of over 400 prior analyses
Managerial implications	Long-term sales growth for a brand is derived mainly from category growth. While temporary share gains and losses are common, it is difficult to generate sustained long-term market-share growth in mature markets.
Contributors	Marnik G. Dekimpe, Tilburg University and Catholic University of Leuven, and Dominique M. Hanssens, UCLA
Reference	Dekimpe, Marnik G., and Dominique M. Hanssens (1995), "Empirical Generalizations About Market Evolution and Stationarity." *Marketing Science* 14 (3) (Part 2 of 2), G109–21

Market Share and Profitability

Profitability is not a direct function of market share. While the average weighted market share–profit elasticity is .35, when factors such as intangibles (e.g., brands, customer relationships, intellectual property, etc.) are also modeled, the elasticity is reduced to zero.

Evidence base	Meta-analysis of 276 prior studies
Managerial implications	Profit and market share are each simultaneously positively driven by intangibles, goods/service quality, product line breadth, sales force expenditures, and the growth of the market. Thus, improvements in any of these areas can expand both share and profitability. Attempts at increasing market share alone may not yield greater profitability.
Contributors	David Szymanski, Texas A&M University, Sundar Bharadwaj, Emory University, and P. Rajan Varadarajan, Texas A&M University
Reference	Szymanski, David M., Sundar G. Bharadwaj, and P. Rajan Varadarajan (1993), "An Analysis of the Market Share-Profitability Relationship." *Journal of Marketing* 57 (3), 1–18

Market Leadership

Of the leading brands in 1923, more failed than remained market leaders by 1997. Of the top three brands in 1923, more failed than remained among the top five brands in 1997. Market-share ranks over this prolonged period are not stable. Non-durable goods have higher leadership persistence and a lower failure rate than durable goods. Brand leaders in food and beverages perform above average and brand leaders in clothing perform below average.

Evidence base	650 brands in 100 categories over seven decades
Managerial implications	Over extended periods, leading brands face a meaningful risk of losing their market leadership. Therefore, companies with leading brands must continue to monitor and invest in them. Companies without leading brands should continuously evaluate selective brand investments aimed at supplanting current leaders.
Contributor	Peter N. Golder, New York University
Reference	Golder, Peter N. (2000), "Historical Method in Marketing Research with New Evidence on Long-Term Market Share Stability." *Journal of Marketing Research* 37 (2), 156–72

Brand Geography: Concentration

Even in the largest geographic markets the largest firm typically has at least a 20% share of the volume sold. Within a category, one or two advertising-supported brands typically dominate each geographic market regardless of market size. Within a category, eight or nine non-advertising brands typically operate in a geographic market, with the number escalating as market size increases.

Evidence base	Monthly data for 31 CPG product categories across the 50 largest ACNielsen SCANTRACKs from 1993 to 1996
Managerial implications	Competition is driven more by the intensity of marketing efforts (e.g., advertising) by a few large firms than by the sheer number of firms competing in a given category and geographic market. While larger, dominant firms must compete with heavier marketing investments, smaller brands can still survive without such investments by catering to consumers who are unwilling to pay a premium for branded goods.
Contributors	Bart J. Bronnenberg, Tilburg University, and Jean-Pierre H. Dubé, University of Chicago
References	Bronnenberg, Bart J., Sanjay K. Dhar, and Jean-Pierre Dubé (2007), "Consumer Packaged Goods in the United States: National Brands, Local Branding." *Journal of Marketing Research* 44 (1), 4–13
	Bronnenberg, Bart J., Sanjay Dhar, and Jean-Pierre Dubé (2008), "Brand History, Geography and the Persistence of CPG Brand Shares." Chicago, Ill.: University of Chicago, Working Paper
	Bronnenberg, Bart J., Sanjay Dhar, and Jean-Pierre Dubé (2008), "Endogenous Sunk Costs and the Geographic Differences in the Market Structures of CPG Categories." Chicago, Ill.: University of Chicago, Working Paper

Brand Geography: Geographic Distances

For consumer packaged goods, the geographic component of variance in a brand's share is considerably larger than the time-series component. Across 62 brands, the average R^2 for market fixed-effects is over 80% and the average R^2 for time fixed-effects for a three-year time horizon is less than 5%. There is high dispersion in a given brand's share across geographic markets (average coefficient of variation is .72) and perceived quality across geographic markets (average coefficient of variation is .21). The identities of local leaders in a category differ across geographic markets. Among the set of national brand leaders across categories, a brand leads in at most 64% of the geographic markets. Across categories, on average, eight different brands are share leaders in at least one geographic market.

Evidence base	Consumer packaged goods: monthly data for the two leading national brands in each of 31 CPG categories across the 50 largest ACNielsen SCANTRACKs over a three-year horizon
Managerial implications	Managers devote most of their attention to time-series variation within a market. For example, promotions are justifiable because of their high correlation with shares over time. However, the findings above indicate that geographic variation in shares is much larger than time-series variation. Managers ought to focus their attention on marketing investments that help them understand these enormous cross-market differences. The large geographic differences— not only in shares but in a category's underlying market structure— suggest that marketing strategy may need to be decentralized to adapt to different geographic conditions.
Contributors	Bart J. Bronnenberg, Tilburg University, and Jean-Pierre H. Dubé, University of Chicago
References	Bronnenberg, Bart J., Sanjay K. Dhar, and Jean-Pierre Dubé (2007), "Consumer Packaged Goods in the United States: National Brands, Local Branding." *Journal of Marketing Research* 44 (1), 4–13

Bronnenberg, Bart J., Sanjay Dhar, and Jean-Pierre Dubé (2008), "Brand History, Geography and the Persistence of CPG Brand Shares." Chicago, Ill.: University of Chicago, Working Paper

Bronnenberg, Bart J., Sanjay Dhar, and Jean-Pierre Dubé (2008), "Endogenous Sunk Costs and the Geographic Differences in the Market Structures of CPG Categories." Chicago, Ill.: University of Chicago, Working Paper

Brand Geography: Persistence

For consumer packaged goods, the historic order of entry of the current largest surviving brands predicts the rank order of their current shares in a geographic market. On average, a mature (90 years) CPG brand's share in its most geographically remote market is roughly 20 points lower than its share in its city of origin. Brand shares correlate with advertising across markets, but not with promotional variables.

Likely explanations of such persistence include early mover advantage (most CPG brands studied were launched in the late 19th or early 20th centuries), subsequent preemptive marketing (advertising), and/or distribution investments and enduring consumer brand-buying habits.

Evidence base	Monthly scanner data from ACNielsen (SCANTRACK level and account level) and IRI (BehaviorScan level); historic data on brand roll-out from company archives, published business histories, public archives, and the Internet; and brand quality measures from Young & Rubicam
Managerial implications	This persistence in geographic market share variation is consistent with product innovation and advertising having a greater long-term impact on market share than do pricing and trade promotions. After a major innovation, the entry "clock" can be reset. In the absence of such innovation, however, order of entry may largely determine subsequent market share.
Contributors	Bart J. Bronnenberg, Tilburg University, and Jean-Pierre H. Dubé, University of Chicago
References	Bronnenberg, Bart J., Sanjay K. Dhar, and Jean-Pierre Dubé (2007), "Consumer Packaged Goods in the United States: National Brands, Local Branding." *Journal of Marketing Research* 44 (1), 4–13

Bronnenberg, Bart J., Sanjay Dhar, and Jean-Pierre Dubé (2008), "Brand History, Geography and the Persistence of CPG Brand Shares." Chicago, Ill.: University of Chicago, Working Paper

Bronnenberg, Bart J., Sanjay Dhar, and Jean-Pierre Dubé (2008), "Endogenous Sunk Costs and the Geographic Differences in the Market Structures of CPG Categories." Chicago, Ill.: University of Chicago, Working Paper

6

Order of Entry

Pioneer Survival Rates

For industrial goods businesses, market pioneers tend to have higher survival rates than later entrants. This result is not supported when pioneering a really new product-market, which accounts for 25% of innovations.

Evidence base	264 new industrial product-markets from the *Thomas Register of American Manufacturers*
Managerial implications	While first-mover advantages help a market pioneer survive, these advantages are offset by the market and technological uncertainties associated with pioneering a really new market. For market pioneers, the overall risk-and-return profile is more encouraging for incremental innovation markets. This is because incrementally new products are typically developed in response to an already existing felt need and they tend to be based on a refinement or extension of existing technology. Hence, pioneers in incremental innovation markets have relatively low risk and higher pioneer survival rates.
Contributors	Manohar U. Kalwani, Purdue University, and William T. Robinson, Purdue University
References	Min, Sungwook, Manohar U. Kalwani, and William T. Robinson (2006), "Market Pioneer and Early Follower Survival Risks: A Contingency Analysis of Really New Versus Incrementally New Product-Markets." *Journal of Marketing* 70 (1), 15–33
	Robinson, William T., and Sungwook Min (2002), "Is the First to Market the First to Fail? Empirical Evidence for Industrial Goods Businesses." *Journal of Marketing Research* 39 (1), 120–8

Pioneering in B-to-B

For manufacturing businesses that survive, market pioneers tend to have higher market shares than later entrants.

Evidence base	Major markets in North America, the Asia Pacific region, and Europe. The North American results are based on nine research studies; the other results are based on 2,419 firms in nine countries.
Managerial implications	For market pioneers that survive, their innovation efforts are often rewarded with a higher market share. Pioneer product line breadth advantages are more sustainable than either product quality advantages or patent protection. Thus, when a market pioneer develops a broad product line early, it can force later entrants to serve narrow market niches.
Contributors	Manohar U. Kalwani, Purdue University, and William T. Robinson, Purdue University
References	Kalyanaram, Gurumurthy, William T. Robinson, and Glen L. Urban (1995), "Order of Market Entry: Established Empirical Generalizations, Emerging Empirical Generalizations, and Future Research." *Marketing Science* 14 (3) (Part 2 of 2), G212–21
	Song, X. Michael, C. Anthony Di Benedetto, and Yuzhen Lisa Zhao (1999), "Pioneering Advantages in Manufacturing and Service Industries: Empirical Evidence from Nine Countries." *Strategic Management Journal* 20 (9), 811–35

Order of Entry and Market Share

On average, a pioneer has a 4.2% point advantage in market share over a later entrant. This effect is larger for strategic business units than for brands. The effect size is inflated when product line breadth and marketing expenditures are not included in the model. The effect size is lower when entry is measured in actual sequence, and not aggregated pioneer/non-pioneer.

Evidence base	Meta-analysis of 23 studies providing 64 elasticities from prior analyses
Managerial implications	Entering markets as a pioneer pays off in terms of market share advantage, especially for strategic business units. Pioneering advantages are augmented by service quality, vertical integration, R&D expenditures, shared facilities and customers, market growth, and frequently purchased products.
Contributors	David Szymanski, Texas A&M University, Lisa Troy, Texas A&M University, and Sundar Bharadwaj, Emory University
Reference	Szymanski, David M., Lisa C. Troy, and Sundar G. Bharadwaj (1995), "Order of Entry and Business Performance: An Empirical Synthesis and Reexamination." *Journal of Marketing* 59 (4), 17–33

Order of Entry: Consumer Packaged Goods and Pharmaceuticals

For consumer packaged goods and prescription anti-ulcer drugs, the entrant's forecasted market share divided by the first entrant's market share roughly equals 1 divided by the square root of the order of market entry.

Evidence base	129 consumer brands and 189 monthly observations from the anti-ulcer market (8 brands)
Managerial implications	In these markets, specific share-decline penalties for late entry can be estimated by the 1 over the square root of N rule (where N is the order of entry, $N = 2, 3, \ldots$). These penalties can be reduced by increased advertising and sales expenditures and better product performance and positioning.
Contributor	Glen L. Urban, MIT
References	Kalyanaram, Gurumurthy, and Glen Urban (1992), "Dynamic Effects of the Order of Entry on Market Share, Trial Penetration, and Repeat Purchases for Frequently Purchased Consumer Goods." *Marketing Science* 11 (3), 235–50
	Urban, Glen, Ernst R. Berndt, Linda T. Bui, and David H. Reiley (1997), "The Roles of Marketing, Product Quality and Price Competition in the Growth and Composition of the U.S. Anti-Ulcer Drug Industry." In *The Economics of New Goods*, eds. Timothy Bresnahan and Robert J. Gordan. Chicago, Ill.: University of Chicago Press for the National Bureau of Economic Research
	Urban, Glen L., Theresa Carter, Steven Gaskin, and Zofia Mucha (1986), "Market Share Rewards to Pioneering Brands: An Empirical Analysis and Strategic Implications." *Management Science* 32 (6), 645–59

Order of Entry: Mature Consumer and Industrial Goods

For mature consumer and industrial goods, there is a negative relationship between order of market entry and market share.

Evidence base	Analysis of 129 consumer brands over 36 categories and PIMS data for 1,209 industrial and 371 consumer businesses
Managerial implications	Later entrants should expect a lower share if they introduce similar products to successful pioneers. These penalties can be reduced by increased advertising and sales expenditures and better product performance and positioning.
Contributor	Glen L. Urban, MIT
References	Kalyanaram, Gurumurthy, and Glen Urban (1992), "Dynamic Effects of the Order of Entry on Market Share, Trial Penetration, and Repeat Purchases for Frequently Purchased Consumer Goods." *Marketing Science* 11 (3), 235–50
	Robinson, William T. (1988), "Sources of Market Pioneer Advantages: The Case of Industrial Goods Industries." *Journal of Marketing Research* 25 (1), 87–94
	_____, and Claes Fornell (1985), "Sources of Market Pioneer Advantages in Consumer Goods Industries." *Journal of Marketing Research* 22 (3), 305–17
	Urban, Glen L., Theresa Carter, Steven Gaskin, and Zofia Mucha (1986), "Market Share Rewards to Pioneering Brands: An Empirical Analysis and Strategic Implications." *Management Science* 32 (6), 645–59

Order-of-Entry Effects

The impact of order of entry on long-term market performance is mixed. An initial entrant has a significant market share advantage, with subsequent entrants' share about 1 divided by the square root of the order of entry. This effect declines over time and it is not as strong (although it remains significant) if (1) the reasons that explain these effects are included in the analysis, i.e., considering entry time as endogenous and (2) one accounts for survival bias. However, these effects are explained almost entirely by asymmetries in marketing mix effectiveness. There is no evidence of order-of-entry effect on the long-term survival rate. Pioneers have a short-term profit advantage but a disadvantage in the long term (the production and SG&A cost disadvantage overcome the purchasing advantages).

Evidence base	PIMS data (Robinson and Fornell 1985; Moore et al. 1991; Boulding and Christen 2003); 5 durable and non-durable categories (Urban et al. 1986; Bowman and Gatignon 1996); 50 durable and non-durable categories (Golder and Tellis 1993)
Managerial implications	There is a significant advantage in terms of market share for entering markets early but subsequent entrants can overcome their disadvantage through innovation and marketing. The pioneer must be ready to accept higher costs in the long term.
Contributors	Hubert Gatignon, INSEAD, and Douglas Bowman, Emory University
References	**Main effect of pioneering or order of entry:** Kalyanaram, Gurumurthy, William T. Robinson, and Glen L. Urban (1995), "Order of Market Entry: Established Empirical Generalizations, Emerging Empirical Generalizations, and Future Research." *Marketing Science* 14 (3) (Part 2 of 2), G212–21

Robinson, William T., and Claes Fornell (1985), "Sources of Market Pioneer Advantages in Consumer Goods Industries." *Journal of Marketing Research* 22 (3), 305–17 |

Urban, Glen L., Theresa Carter, Steven Gaskin, and Zofia Mucha (1986), "Market Share Rewards to Pioneering Brands: An Empirical Analysis and Strategic Implications." *Management Science* 32 (6), 645–59

Market entry time is not exogenous:
Boulding, William, and Markus Christen (2003), "Sustainable Pioneering Advantage? Profit Implications of Market Entry Order." *Marketing Science* 22 (3), 371–92

Moore, Michael J., William Boulding, and Ronald C. Goodstein (1991), "Pioneering and Market Share: Is Entry Time Endogenous and Does It Matter?" *Journal of Marketing Research* 28 (1), 97–104

Accounting for survivor bias:
Golder, Peter N., and Gerard J. Tellis (1993), "Pioneer Advantage: Marketing Logic or Marketing Legend?" *Journal of Marketing Research* 30 (2), 158–70

VanderWerf, Pieter A., and John F. Mahon (1997), "Meta-Analysis of the Impact of Research Methods on Findings of First-Mover Advantage." *Management Science* 43 (11), 1510–9

Main effect of entry time is largely as a moderator of marketing mix effectiveness:
Bowman, Douglas, and Hubert Gatignon (1996), "Order of Entry as a Moderator of the Effect of the Marketing Mix on Market Share." *Marketing Science* 15 (3), 222–42

First-mover Advantage

In really new product categories, market pioneers' failure rate is 64%, with an average long-run market share of 6% and leadership incidence of 9%. Instead of first-mover advantage, the superior performance of enduring market leaders is driven by five other factors: vision of the mass market, managerial persistence, relentless innovation, financial commitment, and asset leverage.

Evidence base	66 product categories: 24 digital, high technology, 41 business-to-consumer, 25 combined business-to-business and business-to-consumer
Managerial implications	Companies should not rely on possible first-mover advantages for their success. Instead, first movers and later entrants should focus on identifying a mass market, continuous innovation, and persistent application of resources to achieve and sustain market leadership.
Contributors	Peter N. Golder, New York University, and Gerard J. Tellis, University of Southern California
References	Golder, Peter N., and Gerard J. Tellis (1993), "Pioneer Advantage: Marketing Logic or Marketing Legend." *Journal of Marketing Research* 30 (2), 158–70
	Tellis, Gerard J., and Peter N. Golder (2001), *Will and Vision: How Latecomers Grow to Dominate Markets*. New York, N.Y.: McGraw Hill

7

Sales Takeoff and Diffusion

Adoption/Diffusion Pattern of New Durables

In the Bass diffusion model, the average coefficient of innovation (p) is .03 and the average coefficient of imitation (q) is .30. The values p and q differ by product, with q typically higher for industrial products. The value p is stable over time, while q may be increasing.

Evidence base	Meta-analysis of 213 diffusion models reported in 15 articles published in the 1970s and the 1980s. Most were consumer durables.
Managerial implications	Sales to first-time buyers will peak five to six years from the start of substantial sales.
Contributor	Donald R. Lehmann, Columbia University
Reference	Sultan, Fareena, John U. Farley, and Donald R. Lehmann (1990), "A Meta-Analysis of Applications of Diffusion Models." *Journal of Marketing Research* 27 (1), 70–7

Global Diffusion

The reported mean value of the coefficient of innovation (p), from meta-analysis studies, is .03. It is higher for developed than developing countries and for European countries than for the U.S. The reported mean value of the coefficient of imitation (q), from meta-analysis studies, is .40. It is higher for developing countries than developed countries and for industrial/medical innovations than for durables and other products.

Evidence base	Several published reports on meta-analyses of estimates of the Bass diffusion model
Managerial implications	The diffusion process is affected by word-of-mouth to a larger extent than by innate innovativeness of consumers. Diffusion speed is faster in developed countries than developing countries. It may be best to launch new products earlier in developed countries than in developing countries.
Contributors	Deepa Chandrasekaran, Lehigh University, and Gerard J. Tellis, University of Southern California
References	Chandrasekaran, Deepa, and Tellis, Gerard J. (2007), "A Critical Review of Marketing Research on Diffusion of New Products." In *Review of Marketing Research*, ed. Naresh Malhotra, Vol. 3, 39–81. Armonk, N.Y.: M.E.Sharpe Inc. Sultan, Fareena, John U. Farley, and Donald Lehmann (1990), "A Meta-Analysis of Applications of Diffusion Models." *Journal of Marketing Research* 27 (1), 70–7 Talukdar, Debabrata, K. Sudhir, and Andrew Ainslie (2002), "Investigating New Product Diffusion Across Products and Countries." *Marketing Science* 21 (1), 97–114

Van den Bulte, Christophe, and Stefan Stremersch (2004), "Social Contagion and Income Heterogeneity in New Product Diffusion: A Meta-Analytic Test." *Marketing Science* 23 (4), 530–44

International Diffusion

The average penetration potential for developing countries is about one-third (.17 versus .52) of that for developed countries. It takes developing countries on average 17.9% more time to achieve peak sales (19.25 years versus 16.3 years). Thus, despite the well-known positive effect of product introduction delays on diffusion speed, developing countries still experience a slower adoption rate, compared to that of developed countries.

Several macro-environmental variables influence penetration potential and speed. For example, a 1% change in international trade changes the penetration potential by about .5%. A similar growth in urbanization level changes the penetration potential by .2%.

Evidence base	Data on six new product launches (VCR, CD, microwaves, camcorders, faxes, and cellphones) in 31 countries between 1975 and 1997
Managerial implications	Managers can use this information to fine-tune their expectations about diffusion in different countries as they roll out new product launches, and to better predict the demand over multiple years.
Contributor	Andrew Ainslie, UCLA
Reference	Talukdar, Debabrata, Andrew Ainslie, and K. Sudhir (2002), "Investigating New Product Diffusion Across Products and Countries." *Marketing Science* 21 (1), 97–114

Sales Takeoff

The early sales histories of really new consumer durables exhibit consistent regularities including a sharp sales takeoff after 12 years on average (6 years for more recent categories) and a slowdown after an additional 8 years. At takeoff, average sales increase by 428% and market penetration is 2.9%. At slowdown, sales tend to decrease by 15% and market penetration is 34%. Product categories with larger sales increases at takeoff tend to have larger sales declines at slowdown.

Evidence base	31 really new consumer durables (household appliances and consumer electronics) for takeoff and 30 similar categories for slowdown
Managerial implications	Previous sales patterns provide useful benchmarks for today's new product categories. The extended time-to-takeoff requires patience and careful planning. An unusually long time-to-takeoff may indicate that the new product should be withdrawn. Managers should expect a decrease in sales about eight years after takeoff and plan for this slowdown by adjusting manufacturing, sales force, inventory, and marketing.
Contributors	Peter N. Golder, New York University, and Gerard J. Tellis, University of Southern California
References	Golder, Peter N., and Gerard J. Tellis (1997), "Will It Ever Fly? Modeling the Takeoff of Really New Consumer Durables." *Marketing Science* 16 (3), 256–70
	Golder, Peter N., and Gerard J. Tellis (2004), "Growing, Growing, Gone: Cascades, Diffusion, and Turning Points in the Product Life Cycle." *Marketing Science* 23 (2), 207–18

Global Takeoff

The mean time-to-takeoff varies considerably between developed countries (about 7 years) and developing countries (about 12 years). Fun products (information and entertainment) take off faster than work products (home appliances). The mean time-to-takeoff for fun products is about 7 years while the mean time-to-takeoff for work products is about 12 years, across all countries. In developed countries, the mean time-to-takeoff for fun products is about 4 years, and about 8 years for work products. Within Europe, Scandinavian (Nordic) countries see the fastest takeoff, with estimates of takeoff at about 4 years for fun products and about 7 years for work products. Time-to-takeoff is converging over time, at least for developed countries.

Evidence base	16 new products (household appliances, consumer electronics, and communication services) across 31 countries plus 10 products (household appliances, consumer electronics) across 16 European countries
Managerial implications	Distinct cross-country differences in takeoff point to the need for a waterfall entry strategy (staggering the commercialization of new products across countries). It may be best to launch new products in small quick-takeoff countries, to serve as the starting point of the waterfall strategy. This approach lowers risk, provides for learning, and enables seeding of the diffusion process.
Contributors	Deepa Chandrasekaran, Lehigh University, and Gerard J. Tellis, University of Southern California
References	Chandrasekaran, Deepa, and Gerard J. Tellis (2008), "Global Takeoff of New Products: Culture, Wealth, or Vanishing Differences? *Marketing Science* 27 (5), 844–60
	Tellis, Gerard J., Stefan Stremersch, and Eden Yin (2003), "The International Takeoff of New Products: The Role of Economics, Culture, and Country Innovativeness." *Marketing Science* 22 (2), 188–208

Technological Evolution

Contrary to the theory of S-curves, technologies do not show evidence of a single S-shaped curve of performance improvement. Rather, they evolve through a series of steps with steep jumps in performance interspersed with periods of no improvement. Performance of new technologies at the time of launch may be higher or lower than the performance of old technologies. The performance paths of a pair of competing technologies rarely have a single crossing. The rate of technological change and the rate of introduction of new technologies increase over time. New technologies come as much from new entrants as from large incumbents. Most new technologies introduce a sequence of random, seemingly unpredictable secondary dimensions as a new basis of competition.

Evidence base	23 technologies from six markets encompassing 1,004 technology years
Managerial implications	1. Using the S-curve to predict the performance of a technology is quite risky. The continuous emergence of new technologies and the steady growth of most technologies suggest that relying on the status quo is dangerous for any firm.
	2. Attack from below remains a viable threat.
	3. Emergence of secondary dimensions of competition is a significant threat to incumbents.
	4. First-mover advantages may not be lasting because entrants introduce even more innovations than do incumbent firms.
Contributors	Ashish Sood, Emory University, and Gerard J. Tellis, University of Southern California
References	Sood, Ashish, and Gerard J. Tellis (2005), "The S-Curve of Technological Evolution: Strategic Law or Self-Fulfilling Prophecy?" Cambridge, Mass.: Marketing Science Institute, Report No. 04–116
	Sood, Ashish, and Gerard J. Tellis (2005), "Technological Evolution and Radical Innovation." *Journal of Marketing* 69 (3), 152–68

Radical Innovations

Radical innovations take about 50 years, on average, to go from initial concept to broad-market sales. For more recent products, this duration is still 22 years. During this period, different firms tend to lead product and market development for each innovation. For example, 76% of firms that were first to commercialize an innovation were not first to commercialize it to a broader market.

Evidence base	29 radical innovations tracked from initial concept to broad market commercialization (i.e., annual sales of at least 10,000 units). Innovations were commercialized between 1838 and 1983.
Managerial implications	Early-stage investments in radical innovations are not likely to have short-run payoffs. Companies should look externally at existing concepts and prototypes for opportunities to commercialize future radical innovations.
Contributors	Peter N. Golder, New York University, Rachel Shacham, New York University, and Debanjan Mitra, University of Florida
Reference	Golder, Peter N., Rachel Shacham, and Debanjan Mitra (2009), "Innovations' Origins: When, by Whom, and How Are Radical Innovations Developed?" *Marketing Science* 28 (1), 166–79

Cross-country Differences in the Shape of the New Product Diffusion Curve

A country's culture and income distribution are related to the extent to which new products diffuse in that country according to a pronounced S-curve, measured as a higher q/p shape parameter of the Bass diffusion curve.

Specifically, using the Hofstede scale for cultural orientation and the Gini coefficient for income inequality:

■ For products without competing standards, higher individualism and higher uncertainty avoidance lower the q/p ratio. Higher power distance and higher masculinity increase the q/p ratio. For products with competing standards, culture does not affect the q/p ratio.

■ Higher income inequality increases the q/p ratio when there are no competing standards, but lowers the q/p ratio in the presence of competing standards.

Evidence base	Meta-analysis of 293 diffusion trajectories pertaining to 52 consumer durables in 28 countries reported in 46 publications
Managerial implications	A pronounced diffusion curve (slow initial adoption followed by rapid growth) can be predicted from a country's cultural orientation and income inequality. However, the effects depend on whether the product category has competing standards or not (e.g., Betamax vs. VHS in VCRs).
Contributor	Christophe Van den Bulte, University of Pennsylvania
Reference	Van den Bulte, Christophe, and Stefan Stremersch (2004), "Social Contagion and Income Heterogeneity in New Product Diffusion: A Meta-Analytic Test." *Marketing Science* 23 (Fall), 530–44

Competing Standards and the Shape of the New Product Diffusion Curve

Product categories exhibiting competing standards tend to have diffusion trajectories with a more pronounced S-shape. Specifically, the presence of competing standards tends to increase the q/p shape parameter of the Bass diffusion curve by a factor of 2 to 3 and the logistic growth parameter by a factor of 2 to 2.5.

Evidence base	Meta-analysis of 293 diffusion trajectories pertaining to 52 consumer durables in 28 countries reported in 46 publications, and analysis of 31 consumer durables in the U.S.
Managerial implications	The presence of competing standards dramatically slows down early sales growth, but this is compensated by faster growth subsequently.
Contributor	Christophe Van den Bulte, University of Pennsylvania
References	Van den Bulte, Christophe (2000), "New Product Diffusion Acceleration: Measurement and Analysis." *Marketing Science* 19 (Fall), 366–80
	Van den Bulte, Christophe, and Stefan Stremersch (2004), "Social Contagion and Income Heterogeneity in New Product Diffusion: A Meta-Analytic Test." *Marketing Science* 23 (Fall), 530–44

Cross-time Differences in the Shape of the New Product Diffusion Curve

Over the last 50 years, diffusion trajectories have tended to become less S-shaped, as reflected in the q/p shape parameter of Bass diffusion curves trending downward. Specifically, for every 1-year increment in the launch time of a new product, the q/p shape parameter tends to decrease by .1%.

Evidence base	Meta-analysis of 293 diffusion trajectories pertaining to 52 consumer durables in 28 countries reported in 46 publications
Managerial implications	The extent to which new product sales growth is slow at first and accelerates only later has decreased over time and is likely to continue doing so.
Contributor	Christophe Van den Bulte, University of Pennsylvania
Reference	Van den Bulte, Christophe, and Stefan Stremersch (2004), "Social Contagion and Income Heterogeneity in New Product Diffusion: A Meta-Analytic Test." *Marketing Science* 23 (Fall), 530–44

Cross-time Differences in the Speed of New Product Diffusion

Over the last 50 years, the speed of diffusion has increased by about 2–3% a year. Demographic changes and increasing disposable income per household can explain much of this increase.

Evidence base	Analysis of 31 consumer durables in the U.S. (1923–1996) using the logistic diffusion model, and meta-analysis of 188 different product-country combinations (1950–1992) using the Bass model
Managerial implications	New product diffusion cycles have shortened markedly over time. They need not keep doing so, depending on changes in demographic and economic trends.
Contributor	Christophe Van den Bulte, University of Pennsylvania
References	Van den Bulte, Christophe (2002), "Want to Know How Diffusion Speed Varies across Countries and Products? Try Using a Bass Model." *PDMA Visions* 26 (4), 12–5
	Van den Bulte, Christophe, and Stefan Stremersch (2004), "Social Contagion and Income Heterogeneity in New Product Diffusion: A Meta-Analytic Test." *Marketing Science* 23 (Fall), 530–44

8

Product Innovation

Innovation Generation

The key drivers of innovation and their effect sizes are past innovation (effect size = .47), openness to change (effect size = .36), presence of innovation champions (effect size = .29), customer orientation (effect size = .25), intelligence generation (effect size = .23), and extent of professionalism (effect size = .23). Innovation drives firm performance on average (effect size = .09), while radical innovation has a more significant effect on firm performance (effect size = .25), and incremental innovation has a much smaller effect (effect size = .07).

Evidence base	Meta-analysis of 273 prior effect sizes from 187 studies and a sample of 337,470 observations from the period 1970–2007
Managerial implications	Innovation in firms is driven by a history of innovation, organizational resources, processes, and cultural factors. Resources, such as past innovation, diversification, and network relationships, taken together, explain the majority of the variance in innovation generation. Furthermore, an organization's motivation to innovate (i.e., customer and competitor orientation, and openness to change) are also key drivers of innovation generation.
Contributors	Leslie Vincent, University of Kentucky, Sundar Bharadwaj, Emory University, and Goutam Challagalla, Georgia Institute of Technology
Reference	Vincent, Leslie, Sundar Bharadwaj, and Goutam Challagalla (2008), "Antecedents, Consequences, and the Mediating Role of Innovation Generation." Lexington, Kentucky: University of Kentucky, Gatton College of Business and Economics, Working Paper

Product Innovation

There is a U-shaped relation between the degree of newness of a new packaged good product and its success in the marketplace. Products of intermediate newness systematically generate a lower purchase rate during the first year after introduction compared to incrementally new products and true innovations.

Evidence base	Over 500 new product introductions in foods, beverages, personal care, and household care in France, Germany, Spain, the Netherlands, and the U.K.
Managerial implications	Beware of compromises in the new-product development process, which often lead to products that are stuck in the middle. Moderately novel products typically are not much higher in relative advantage compared to incrementally new products, while not much lower in complexity than really new innovations.
Contributor	Jan-Benedict E.M. Steenkamp, University of North Carolina at Chapel Hill
References	Gielens, Katrijn, and Jan-Benedict E.M. Steenkamp (2007), "Drivers of Consumer Acceptance of New Packaged Goods: An Investigation across Products and Countries." *International Journal of Research in Marketing* 24 (2), 97–111 Steenkamp, Jan-Benedict E.M., and Katrijn Gielens (2003), "Consumer and Market Drivers of the Trial Probability of New Consumer Packaged Goods." *Journal of Consumer Research* 30 (3), 368–84

New Product Trial

Several consumer traits predict how likely consumers are to try a new product. Consumer innovativeness has the strongest positive impact on trial probability (relative effect size $s = .23$), followed by usage intensity ($s = .12$) and income ($s = .11$). Consumers who are susceptible to peer influences have a lower trial probability and tend to delay trial ($s = .06$). Market mavenism, a characteristic often mentioned in the context of new products, does not have an overall significant impact. However, some elements of marketing strategy can influence these results as follows:

- The effect of *advertising* is stronger for consumers that score high on market mavenism, and weaker for consumers that score high on innovativeness. Advertising also lessens the negative effect of peer influence.
- The effect of *feature* and *displays* is stronger for consumers that rate high on innovativeness, market mavenism, and usage intensity.
- The effect of the new product's *novelty* (newness) is stronger for consumers that score high on innovativeness and have higher incomes. Product newness also diminishes the positive effect of usage intensity and reinforces the negative impact of peer influence.
- The positive effect of *brand strength* is stronger for consumers that score high on market mavenism and usage intensity.

Evidence base	239 new product introductions in the consumer packaged goods industry in the Netherlands
Managerial implications	Consumer characteristics such as innovativeness, usage intensity, and income offer an actionable basis for segmentation and targeted marketing efforts. These traits can be assessed a priori rather than ex post. Consumers can then be classified according to their scores before new-product introduction, which helps firms decide whom to target and which marketing instruments to use in their launch strategy.
Contributor	Katrijn Gielens, University of North Carolina at Chapel Hill

Reference   Steenkamp, Jan-Benedict E.M., and Katrijn Gielens (2003),
                "Consumer and Market Drivers of the Trial Probability of New
                Consumer Packaged Goods." *Journal of Consumer Research* 30 (3),
                368–84

Competition and New Product Acceptance

New product acceptance is systematically affected by the competitive environment. Consumer acceptance is higher in less concentrated, less heavily promoted, and less heavily advertised categories, and in categories with more intense competition on innovation. Competitive conduct is much more important than competitive structure: the average relative effect size of market concentration is .072, but that of competitive conduct is .509. Thus competitive conduct shapes 50% of the total effect, either by itself, or in combination with product factors.

Negative competitive effects can be significantly reduced by variables under the control of the firm, viz., brand reputation and product newness. Overall, product newness dampens the impact of competitors' price promotion intensity and new product introduction intensity. These two moderating effects of product newness each explain up to 10% of the total effect of the drivers of new product success. Brand reputation has a softening effect on the impact of competitive advertising intensity, accounting for 6% of the total effect.

Evidence base	Over 300 product introductions in the consumer packaged goods industry in four countries (France, Germany, Spain, and the U.K.)
Managerial implications	Insight into the effects of the competitive environment is important in order to develop realistic marketing plans and sales targets. However, the firm introducing the new product does not have to consider competitive influences as completely beyond their control, as product newness and brand strength can be used to successfully counter negative competitive effects.
Contributor	Katrijn Gielens, University of North Carolina at Chapel Hill
Reference	Gielens, Katrijn, and Jan Benedict E.M. Steenkamp, (2007), "Drivers of Consumer Acceptance of New Packaged Goods: An Investigation Across Products and Countries." *International Journal of Research in Marketing* 24 (2), 97–111

New Product Announcements and Stock Prices

The stock market reaction to a product-innovation announcement is, on average, approximately .5% abnormal return (return over and above the expected stock return for the announcing firm).

Evidence base	1,101 *Wall Street Journal* new product announcements, 105 product announcements in the Predicast F&S Index database, and 5,481 announcements from Factiva, Lexis Nexis, and company websites
Managerial implications	All else equal, the market value of firms increases following the announcement of introduction of a new product. This generalization does not suggest that any incremental innovation is a positive net present value project. Rather, new products that are significant enough to warrant a press release by the parent firm are, on average, viewed by investors as increasing the future cash flows of the firm. While abnormal returns to announcements of new products in high tech industries have typically been shown to be higher than .5%, studies across multiple industries (Chaney, Devinney, and Winer 1991; Sood and Tellis 2009) have consistently demonstrated positive abnormal returns following such announcements.
Contributor	Alina Sorescu, Texas A&M University
References	Chaney, Paul K., Timothy M. Devinney, and Russell S. Winer (1991), "The Impact of New Product Introductions on the Market Value of Firms." *Journal of Business* 64 (4), 573–610
	Lee, Hun, Ken G. Smith, Curtis M. Grimm, and August Schomburg (2000), "Timing, Order and Durability of New Product Advantages with Imitation." *Strategic Management Journal* 21 (1), 23–30
	Sood, Ashish, and Gerard J. Tellis (2009), "Do Innovations Really Pay Off? Total Stock Market Returns to Innovation." *Marketing Science,* forthcoming

Long-term Effect of Innovation on Firm Value

The long-term (one-year window) effect of innovation on firm stock market value is significantly positive and is greater for radical than for incremental innovations.

Evidence base	399 innovations introduced by 6 automobile firms; 22,532 innovations introduced by 153 consumer packaged goods firms
Managerial implications	All else equal, innovation has a persistent, long-term positive effect on firm stock market value and this effect is greater for radical than for incremental innovations.
Contributor	Alina Sorescu, Texas A&M University
References	Pauwels, Koen, Jorge Silva-Risso, Shuba Srinivasan, and Dominique M. Hanssens (2004), "New Products, Sales Promotions, and Firm Value: The Case of the Automobile Industry." *Journal of Marketing* 68 (4), 142–56
	Sorescu, Alina, and Jelena Spanjol (2008), "Innovation's Effect on Firm Value and Risk: Insights from Consumer Packaged Goods." *Journal of Marketing* 72 (2), 114–32

9

Price Effects

Price Elasticity

For consumer packaged goods, the average price-to-sales elasticity at the brand level is –2.6. The price elasticity has become stronger (more negative) over the past half century. Price elasticities are stronger (more negative) in the introduction/growth stage than in the mature/decline stage; for durables than for fast-moving consumer goods; at the stock-keeping-unit level than at the brand level; and in market share and choice models than in sales models. In the short run, the promotional price elasticity is larger in magnitude than the actual price elasticity, but the reverse is true in the long run.

Evidence base	Meta-analysis of 1,851 price elasticities across 81 studies
Managerial implications	For consumer packaged goods, price has grown in importance as a determinant of sales since the 1950s. Over time, discounting has become more effective in boosting sales, but raising prices has an increasingly negative impact on sales. When introducing a new product category, a penetration pricing strategy (low to high) is more effective than a skimming price strategy (high to low).
Contributor	Harald J. van Heerde, University of Waikato, New Zealand
Reference	Bijmolt, Tammo H.A., Harald J. van Heerde, and Rik G.M. Pieters (2005), "New Empirical Generalizations on the Determinants of Price Elasticity." *Journal of Marketing Research* 42 (2), 141–56

Reference Price Effects

Reference price effects were found in 92% of 13 studies: 85% reported a reference price effect in brand choice, and 1 of only 2 studies of purchase incidence found an effect. The smoothing parameter for past prices in the formation of reference averages .60, implying that only one to two past prices are salient in reference price formation. The "sticker shock" elasticity to utility in brand choice is 1.3. For example, the base disutility of shelf price of a brand is increased by about 13% for every 10% positive difference between the observed price and the reference price.

Evidence base	Analysis of the results of 13 prior studies covering 20 frequently purchased product categories. Smoothing parameter and "sticker shock" elasticity are based on analysis of parameters reported in Briesch et al. (1997) for 4 product categories.
Managerial implications	Consumers react not only to competitive prices but also compare them favorably or unfavorably in relation to the prices observed on recent purchases. Managers can therefore increase the likelihood of choosing a brand by communicating the brand's price positively relative to its recent past prices.
Contributors	Tridib Mazumdar, Syracuse University, and S. P. Raj, Syracuse University
References	Bell, David R., and James M. Lattin (2000), "Looking for Loss Aversion in Scanner Panel Data: The Confounding Effect of Price Response Heterogeneity." *Marketing Science* 19 (2), 185–200
	Briesch, Richard A., Lakshman Krishnamurthi, Tridib Mazumdar, and S.P. Raj (1997), "A Comparative Analysis of Reference Price Models." *Journal of Consumer Research* 24 (2) 202–14
	Mazumdar, Tridib, S.P. Raj, and Indrajit Sinha (2005), "Reference Price Research: Review and Propositions." *Journal of Marketing* 69 (4), 84–102

Effects of Pricing Periodicity

Variation in brand retail prices
- Price changes over the medium term (price cycle length of 4–13 weeks) and the long term (greater than 13 week cycles) explain most of the variation in supermarket prices of consumer packaged goods. Short-term promotional price changes (2–4 week cycles), such as deals followed by return to regular price, explain the least amount of variation in supermarket prices.
- The dominant frequency of price variation varies systematically with brand and category factors. For example, greater purchase frequency increases the dominant frequency of price variation.

Covariation in retail prices across brands
- Price covariation occurs in multiple frequencies, usually not coinciding with the sample frequency of the data. Like price variation, this depends on brand and category factors.
- Discounts are often staggered across brands whereas regular price changes are often concurrent. Therefore, it is possible to observe no price covariation in aggregate data even when there is substantial price covariation at different frequencies.

Evidence base	Time series analysis across 35 grocery categories, 400 weeks, and a total of 166 brands
Managerial implications	Competitive price interactions depend on the planning cycle of managers and are often obscured when mixed together. Given most models and insights confound regular and discount price changes, managers should consider each factor separately.
Contributors	Bart Bronnenberg, Tilburg University, and Carl Mela, Duke University
Reference	Bronnenberg, Bart J., Carl F. Mela, and William Boulding (2006), "The Periodicity of Pricing." *Journal of Marketing Research* 43 (3), 477–93

Cross-price Impact: Neighborhood Price Effects

In grocery products, brands that are closer to each other in price have greater cross-price effects than brands that are priced farther apart. In particular, brands that are closest to each other in price have an average absolute cross-price effect of .090, while brands that are priced farther apart (fourth closest in price) have an average absolute cross-price effect of .043. This phenomenon is called the "neighborhood price effect." Absolute cross-price effect is measured as the change in market share (percentage) points of a target brand when a competing brand's price changes by 1% of the category price.

Evidence base	Meta-analysis of 1,060 cross-price effects on 280 brands from 19 different grocery product categories
Managerial implications	All else equal, brand managers should carefully monitor the discounts of their closely priced neighboring brands and, if necessary, provide offsetting discounts to avoid loss of sales.
Contributor	Raj Sethuraman, Southern Methodist University
Reference	Sethuraman, Raj, V. Srinivasan, and Doyle Kim (1999), "Asymmetric and Neighborhood Cross-Price Effects: Some Empirical Generalizations." *Marketing Science* 18 (1), 23–41

Cross-price Impact: Asymmetric Price Effects

The average cross-price elasticity of a higher-priced national brand's price cut on a lower-priced store brand's market share is .48, which is higher than the average cross-price elasticity of a lower-priced store brand's price cut on a higher-priced national brand's market share (.34). This phenomenon is called the "asymmetric price effect." However, the average absolute cross-price effect of a higher-priced national brand's price cut on a lower-priced store brand's market share is .07, which is not different from the average absolute cross-price effect of a lower-priced store brand's price cut on the share of the higher-priced national brand (.072).

Evidence base	Meta-analysis of 210 cross-price effects from 105 national brand–store brand pairs
Managerial implications	Conventional belief holds that national brand price cuts hurt store brand sales more than the reverse. This belief implies that national brands have a greater incentive to discount to take share away from store brands than vice versa. However, the conventional belief holds only when cross-price effects are measured in terms of elasticities but not when they are measured in absolute cross-price effects. Therefore, we cannot conclude that national brands have greater incentive to discount to garner store brand sales than vice versa.
Contributor	Raj Sethuraman, Southern Methodist University
References	Blattberg, Robert C., and Kenneth J. Wisniewski (1989), "Price-Induced Patterns of Competition." *Marketing Science* 8 (4), 291–309
	Sethuraman, Raj, V. Srinivasan, and Doyle Kim (1999), "Asymmetric and Neighborhood Cross-Price Effects: Some Empirical Generalizations." *Marketing Science* 18 (1), 23–41

Cross-price Impact: Asymmetric Share Effects

The average absolute cross-price effect of a low-share brand's price cut on the market share of a high-share brand is .069, which is greater than the average absolute cross-price effect of a high-share brand's price cut on the market share of a low-share brand (.043). This phenomenon is called the "asymmetric share effect."

Evidence base	Meta-analysis of 1,060 cross-price effects on 280 brands from 19 different grocery product categories
Managerial implications	All else equal, manufacturers of low-share brands would have a greater incentive to discount because they can attract a larger pool of consumers.
Contributor	Raj Sethuraman, Southern Methodist University
Reference	Sethuraman, Raj, and V. Srinivasan (2002), "The Asymmetric Share Effect: An Empirical Generalization on Cross-Price Effects." *Journal of Marketing Research* 39 (3), 379–86

Private Label Margins

In grocery products, the gross percentage profit margin per unit received by the retailer on the store brand is greater than the retailer's percentage margin on the national brand. One gross margin estimate is 34% for store brands and 24% for national brands. Gross percent margin is the profit contribution computed as a percent of brand price = [(price – variable cost) × 100/price].

Evidence base	Compilation of six academic and industry studies
Managerial implications	The higher gross percentage margin for store brands does not imply that retailers should promote their store brands, nor does it necessarily imply that manufacturers should close the percent margin gap by reducing their wholesale prices. Retailers and manufacturers should consider unit dollar contribution margin (price – variable cost) and profitability per square foot of retail space when making their price and promotion decisions.
Contributor	Raj Sethuraman, Southern Methodist University
References	Sethuraman, Raj (2006), "Private-Label Marketing Strategies in Packaged Goods; Management Beliefs and Research Insights." Cambridge, Mass.: Marketing Science Institute, Report No. 06–108
	Sethuraman, Raj (2009), "Assessing the External Validity of Analytical Results from National Brand and Store Brand Competition Models." *Marketing Science*, forthcoming

Price Stickiness

While changes in demand, cost, and competitive prices do have an effect, past-pricing patterns are the main driver of retail price variation over time (57%). Such price stickiness is related to lower retailer profitability.

Evidence base	24 categories in Dominick's Finer Foods (http://research.chicagobooth.edu/marketing/databases/dominicks/) and 43 categories in Denver (provided by ACNielsen)
Managerial implications	While adjusting prices to changes in demand is associated with higher retailer gross margins, past-price dependence has been linked to lower margins. Retailers' reliance on past prices also has implications for manufacturers. For example, past-price dependence is stronger for smaller brands, making it harder for manufacturers to achieve high levels of trade deal pass-through. More research is needed to quantify the cost of demand-based pricing and to develop strategies to reduce it.
Contributors	Vincent Nijs, Northwestern University, Koen Pauwels, Dartmouth College, and Shuba Srinivasan, Boston University
References	Nijs, Vincent R., Shuba Srinivasan, and Koen Pauwels (2007), "Retail-Price Drivers and Retailer Profits." *Marketing Science* 26 (4), 473–87
	Srinivasan, Shuba, Koen Pauwels, and Vincent Nijs (2008), "Demand-Based Pricing Versus Past-Price Dependence: A Cost-Benefit Analysis." *Journal of Marketing* 72 (2), 15–27

10

Brands and Brand Loyalty

Brand Price Premium

For grocery products, consumers will pay a price premium for national brands even when the quality of the national brands and the store brands is the same. This premium is called the image premium or reputation premium. Price premium is measured as [price willing to pay for national brand – price of store brand] expressed as a percent of national brand price. The average image premium has been estimated at 26%.

Evidence base	20 grocery products, 132 consumer and 78 grocery products, aggregate consumer reports data
Managerial implications	National brand managers can maintain and increase the image premium through advertising and other marketing activities that enhance perceptions of brand equity. Retailers may need to charge a lower price for their store brands (that is, maintain a minimum price differential between national brands and store brands) even if there is no significant perceived quality difference between the two brands.
Contributor	Raj Sethuraman, Southern Methodist University
References	Apelbaum, Eidan, Eitan Gerstner, and Prasad Naik (2003), "The Effects of Expert Quality Evaluations versus Brand Name on Price Premiums." *Journal of Product and Brand Management* 12 (3), 154–65
	Sethuraman, Raj (2000), "What Makes Consumers Pay More for National Brands Than for Store Brands: Image or Quality?" Cambridge, Mass.: Marketing Science Institute Report No. 00–110

Sethuraman, Raj (2003), "Measuring National Brands' Equity over Store Brands." *Review of Marketing Science* 1 (2), 1–26

Private Labels and Store Loyalty

There is an inverted U-shaped relationship between consumers' private label share in a chain and their behavioral loyalty to that chain. Chain loyalty first increases with private label share, but the effect turns negative at private label shares around 35–40%.

Evidence base	Consumer packaged goods: analysis of shoppers at two major retail chains in the U.S. and two major retail chains in the Netherlands
Managerial implications	Private label use increases store loyalty but only up to a point. Beyond that, the effect can be negative, so retailers must have a good balance of national and store brands in order to optimize store traffic, sales, and loyalty.
Contributor	Kusum Ailawadi, Dartmouth College
References	Ailawadi, Kusum, and Bari Harlam (2004), "An Empirical Analysis of the Determinants of Retail Margins: The Role of Store-Brand Share." *Journal of Marketing* 68 (1), 147–65
	Ailawadi, Kusum L., Koen Pauwels, and Jan-Benedict E.M. Steenkamp (2008), "Private-Label Use and Store Loyalty." *Journal of Marketing* 72 (6), 19–30

Brand Loyalty Evolution

Brand loyalty for consumer packaged goods is not systematically declining over time, nor is the short-run variability around a brand's mean loyalty level.

Evidence base	Time-series analysis on monthly or bi-monthly loyalty estimates for 92 brands from 21 frequently purchased consumer goods categories over one to two years
Managerial implications	Managers are often concerned about recurring claims that brand loyalty is gradually eroding. While managers should not become complacent, these claims are largely exaggerated, especially for market-share leaders.
Contributors	Marnik G. Dekimpe, Tilburg University and Catholic University of Leuven, and Jan-Benedict E.M. Steenkamp, University of North Carolina at Chapel Hill
Reference	Dekimpe, Marnik G., Jan-Benedict E.M. Steenkamp, Martin Mellens, and Piet Vanden Abeele (1997), "Decline and Variability in Brand Loyalty." *International Journal of Research in Marketing* 14 (5), 405–20

Private Label Quality

For grocery products, a decrease in the perceived quality differential between a national brand and store brand increases the store brand's unit market share. According to one estimate, a 1% decrease in perceived quality differential between national and store brands increases store brand market share by .3%. This represents a 1.74% increase from the average store brand unit market share of 17.2%.

Evidence base	Estimate based on data from 210 grocery product categories. Generalization based on a compilation of 16 academic and industry studies
Managerial implications	Quality has been found to be an important consideration for private label purchases (sometimes even more important than price). Retailers should generally emphasize quality in their product development and promotion of private labels. Manufacturers should attempt to differentiate their national brands on quality.
Contributor	Raj Sethuraman, Southern Methodist University
References	Hoch, Stephen J., and Shumeet Banerji (1993), "When Do Private Labels Succeed?" *Sloan Management Review* 34 (4), 57–67
	Sethuraman, Raj (2006), "Private-Label Marketing Strategies in Packaged Goods: Management Beliefs and Research Insights." Cambridge, Mass.: Marketing Science Institute Report No. 06–108

11

Price Promotions

Retail Promotion Pass-through

For manufacturers who provide trade promotion funds and receive promotion spending by retailers, the median pass-through rate by retailers is 65–75%. Pass-through is greater than 100% for 10–25% of manufacturers. Pass-through is higher for large-share manufacturers and in high-sales product categories.

Evidence base	Consumer packaged goods: Analysis of promotion spending by two U.S. retail chains across multiple product categories (25 categories sold by one chain and all categories sold by the other chain)
Managerial implications	There is wide variation in pass-through rates across product categories and across manufacturers. Manufacturers must understand the drivers of retail promotion decisions and design win-win trade promotions that are most likely to be passed through.
Contributor	Kusum Ailawadi, Dartmouth College
References	Ailawadi, Kusum, and Bari Harlam (2009), "Retailer Promotion Pass-Through: A Measure, Its Magnitude, and Its Determinants." *Marketing Science*, forthcoming
	Besanko, David, Jean-Pierre Dubé, and Sachin Gupta (2005), "Own-Brand and Cross-Brand Retail Pass-Through." *Marketing Science* 24 (1), 123–37

Channel Pass-through of Trade Promotions

For one consumer packaged goods category, pass-through elasticities average .71 for the wholesaler, .59 for the retailer, and .42 for the channel. As an example, a 10% reduction in manufacturer price would result in a 4.2% consumer price reduction.

Evidence base	Two years of data on prices, shipments, sales, and promotions for the distribution channel (i.e., manufacturer, wholesaler, and retailer) in a major consumer packaged goods category in over 30 U.S. states
Managerial implications	Manufacturers and retailers have debated the level of trade-deal pass-through for decades. The profitability of manufacturer and wholesaler deals can be improved by utilizing detailed effectiveness estimates. For example, a manufacturer using an inclusive trade-deal strategy might offer a 10% off-invoice deal to all retailers on every product. This strategy would decrease manufacturer and wholesaler profits for 56% of product/store combinations, while retailers would experience a profit boost in 96% of cases.
	Manufacturers and wholesalers can avoid unprofitable trade deals for specific products and retailers by utilizing accurate estimates of pass-through, consumer demand elasticity, and margins. Such a selective trade-deal strategy could improve deal profitability by up to 86% and reduce costs by 40%. Although total retailer profits would drop by 51%, retailers receiving deals could still see a profit boost in 95% of cases.
Contributors	Vincent Nijs, Northwestern University, and Kanishka Misra, Northwestern University
Reference	Nijs, Vincent R., Kanishka Misra, Eric Anderson, Karsten Hansen, and Lakshman Krishnamurthi (2009), "Channel Pass-Through of Trade Promotions." *Marketing Science*, forthcoming

Category-Demand Effects of Price Promotions

In the majority of cases (58%) price promotions significantly expand the size of a category, with a net elasticity (2.21) that is accumulated over a period of 10 weeks on average. Persistent category-demand effects of price promotions are rare (2% of cases).

Evidence base	Four years of data on 560 supermarket product categories in the Netherlands
Managerial implications	Price promotions can increase the size of the pie (category demand), not just the relative size of the slices (market share). To enhance retailer cooperation, manufacturers should demonstrate that promotions can temporarily boost demand for an entire category. Since long-run effects of price promotions are rare, retailers should focus on other marketing instruments, such as new product introductions, to achieve persistent growth.
Contributor	Vincent Nijs, Northwestern University
Reference	Nijs, Vincent R., Marnik G. Dekimpe, Jan-Benedict E.M. Steenkamp, and Dominique M. Hanssens (2001), "The Category-Demand Effects of Price Promotions." *Marketing Science* 20 (1), 1–22

Decomposition of Long-term Sales Promotion Effects

The *total net effect* (expressed in elasticity) of a sales promotion is positive and derives mostly from primary demand expansion (category incidence and purchase quantity), not secondary demand (brand switching). About 60% of the long-term effect is due to higher category incidence; the remaining 40% is mostly captured by brand switching for perishable products, and by increased purchase quantity for storable products. These breakdowns are different from *short-term results*, where the effect is 75% secondary demand (i.e., brand choice) and 25% primary demand (i.e., category incidence and purchase quantity). For storable products, the 25% primary demand expansion is 4% category incidence, 21% purchase quantity. For perishable products, this breakdown is 17% category incidence, 8% purchase quantity.

Evidence base	17 store-brand combinations for a perishable product category and 12 store-brand combinations for a storable category, Sioux Falls, South Dakota, 1986–1988
Managerial implications	Price promotions do not only seduce consumers to switch brands, they also induce them to buy in the category in the first place. Encouraging brand manufacturers to price promote is meaningful for retailers interested in temporary demand expansion of the category.
Contributor	Koen Pauwels, Ozegin University and Dartmouth College
References	Bell, David R., Jeongwen Chiang, and V. Padmanabhan (1999) "The Decomposition of Promotional Response: An Empirical Generalization." *Marketing Science* 18 (4), 504–26
	Gupta, Sunil (1988), "Impact of Sales Promotion on When, What and How Much to Buy." *Journal of Marketing Research* 25 (4), 342–55
	Pauwels, Koen, Dominique Hanssens, and S. Siddarth (2002), "The Long-Term Effects of Price Promotions on Category Incidence, Brand Choice, and Purchase Quantity." *Journal of Marketing Research* 39 (4), 421–39

Price Promotion Elasticity

Since a price promotion leads to a strong temporary sales increase for the promoted brand, a lot of research has focused on where this sales bump comes from. The average price promotion elasticity is –3.63, meaning that 1% promotional price discount leads to a 3.63% increase in brand sales. Research that is based on decomposing this elasticity concludes that brand switching (brand choice elasticity) accounts for the major part of the bump (75%), whereas temporary category growth (purchase incidence and quantity elasticities) comprises the remaining 25%. However, looking at elasticities does not give the full picture, and the opposite conclusion emerges when these results are expressed in unit sales. A promotion leads to "bigger pie": a temporary increase in that week's sales for the entire category. At the same time competitor brands suffer from a "smaller slice of the larger pie": a temporarily lower percentage share. These two counteracting forces mitigate the net loss of sales for competitor brands. As a consequence, a 100-unit promotional sales bump for a brand only leads to a 33-unit (rather than 75-unit) sales loss for competitor brands and a 67-unit (rather than 25-unit) increase in category sales during the promotional week.

Evidence base	(Re-)Analysis of 173 brands across 13 CPG categories
Managerial implications	In terms of unit sales effects, brand switching is a much smaller contributor to the sales bump of a promoted brand (33%) than temporary category growth (67%). Thus, both for retailers and manufacturers, promotions may seem more attractive than the elasticity decomposition suggests. The caveat is that part of the temporary category growth represents consumer stockpiling.
Contributor	Harald J. van Heerde, University of Waikato, New Zealand
References	Bell, David R., Jeongwen Chiang, and V. Padmanabhan (1999), "The Decomposition of Promotional Response: An Empirical Generalization." *Marketing Science* 18 (4), 504–26
	Van Heerde, Harald J., Sachin Gupta, and Dick R. Wittink (2003), "Is 75% of the Sales Promotion Bump Due to Brand Switching? No, Only 33% Is." *Journal of Marketing Research* 40 (4), 481–91

Sales Promotion Effects

Price promotions do not have permanent monetary effects for either the manufacturer or the retailer. Estimates of total (long-run) price-promotion elasticities are 3.70 for brand sales, 2.30 for manufacturer revenue, .50 for category sales at the chain level, 1.40 for category sales at the national level, −.05 for retailer revenue, and −.70 for retailer margins.

Evidence base	Analysis of 25 categories in the U.S. over a seven-year period; analysis of 560 consumer product categories in the Netherlands over a four-year period
Managerial implications	The interests of manufacturers and retailers are not necessarily aligned when it comes to price promotions. Therefore, it is important for each party to scrutinize the conditions under which promotions make money and allocate their scarce marketing dollars toward such cases.
Contributor	Shuba Srinivasan, Boston University
References	Nijs, Vincent R., Marnik G. Dekimpe, Jan-Benedict E.M. Steenkamp, and Dominique M. Hanssens (2001), "The Category-Demand Effects of Price Promotions." *Marketing Science* 20 (1), 1–22
	Pauwels, Koen, and Shuba Srinivasan (2004), "Who Benefits from Store Brand Entry?" *Marketing Science* 23 (3), 364–90
	Srinivasan, Shuba, Koen Pauwels, Dominique Hanssens, and Marnik Dekimpe (2002), "Who Benefits from Price Promotions?" *Harvard Business Review* 80 (9), 22–3
	Srinivasan, Shuba, Koen H. Pauwels, Dominique M. Hanssens, and Marnik G. Dekimpe (2004), "Do Promotions Benefit Manufacturers, Retailers, or Both?" *Management Science* 50 (5), 617–29

Manufacturer Sales Promotions

On average, the net long-term sales effect of a manufacturer sales promotion is 10% higher when there is retailer feature and/or display support, 6% lower when the effects of retailer category management are considered, and 10% lower when brand competitor reaction is included in the analysis.

Evidence base	Across 75 brands in 25 fast-moving consumer product categories
Managerial implications	Price reactions by brand competitors matter, but retailer decisions on category management matter even more!
Contributor	Koen Pauwels, Ozyegin University and Dartmouth College
Reference	Pauwels, Koen (2007), "How Retailer and Competitor Decisions Drive the Long-Term Effectiveness of Manufacturer Promotions for Fast Moving Consumer Goods." *Journal of Retailing* 83 (3), 297–308

12

Personal Selling

Personal Selling Impact

The average personal selling-to-sales (PS) elasticity is about .32. After correcting for methodology-induced biases, the mean corrected (PS) elasticity is .352. This means that an increase of the personal selling effort (budget) by 10% results in an increase of sales by 3.52%. On average, products in the early stages of their life cycles exhibit higher values of PS elasticity, and vice versa. Also, on average, the PS elasticity in European market settings is higher than the PS elasticity in the U.S. Further, PS elasticity estimates from more recent studies are smaller than those from older studies.

Evidence base	Meta-analysis of 46 prior studies providing a total of 3,193 personal selling elasticity measures
Managerial implications	All else equal, companies should invest more in direct sales force resources when launching and establishing new products, while shifting to other means of marketing communication as products mature. Similarly, all else equal, multinational firms should invest more in personal selling efforts in European markets than in U.S. markets. The efficient ratio of personal selling expenditures to total revenues is about 12.5%. Managers can use this ratio as a decision-making benchmark while setting personal selling expenditure levels.
Contributors	Sönke Albers, Christian-Albrechts-University at Kiel, Germany, Murali Mantrala, University of Missouri, and Shrihari Sridhar, University of Missouri
Reference	Albers, Sönke, Murali K. Mantrala, and Shrihari Sridhar (2008), "A Meta-analysis of Personal Selling Elasticities." Cambridge, Mass.: Marketing Science Institute Report No. 08–100

Trade Show Effectiveness

The average elasticity for booth space at trade shows is .162, for booth salespeople it is .884, and for percentage of attendees with buying plans for the types of products exhibited by the firm, it is .128. All else equal, a booth in the IT sector (computers, telecom) draws twice the traffic compared to a booth in other industry sectors (medical, food, construction, and others).

Evidence base	Analyses of 18 years of trade show data covering 50 industries, 164 shows, and nearly 400 firms
Managerial implications	Booth staffing plays a much more significant role in attracting those visitors managers really want (those who have a meaningful engagement with the category) than does the size of the booth itself. Hence, managers should focus on selecting booth staff carefully to improve their company's trade show performance.
Contributors	Srinath Gopalakrishna, University of Missouri, Shrihari (Hari) Sridhar, University of Missouri, Gail R. Buffington, University of Missouri, and Gary L. Lilien, Pennsylvania State University
Reference	Gopalakrishna, Srinath, and Gary L. Lilien (1995), "A Three-Stage Model of Industrial Trade Show Performance." *Marketing Science* 14 (1), 22–42

13

Distribution

Distribution and Market Share

In consumer package goods categories, market share tends to increase with retail distribution at an increasing rate (82% of categories), or otherwise at a proportional (linear) rate (14%). While the elasticity of distribution and market share is thus 1 or higher, retailers also decide on sustainable distribution levels based on product sales. Bulky, low value/space/weight categories generally have higher average ratios of share/distribution as a result of fewer brands being stocked in the average retail store.

Managerial implications	Product-markets have been found to exhibit typical share-distribution curves. For new product introduction, these curves can provide insight into appropriate distribution goals that are contingent on and consistent with share projections.
Evidence base	Analysis of 78,769 stock-keeping units and 49 consumer package goods categories in the U.S., Japan, the Netherlands, and the U.K.
Managerial implications	Retail promotions and slotting fees garner increasing returns at higher levels of weighted retail distribution. Especially when introducing new products, distribution targets should be aligned with market share objectives to ensure that product sales will sustain retail distribution and vice versa.
Contributors	Paul Farris, University of Virginia, David Reibstein, University of Pennsylvania, and Kenneth C. Wilbur, University of Southern California

References

Farris, Paul W., James Olver, and Cornelis De Kluyver (1989), "The Relationship Between Distribution and Market Share." *Marketing Science* 8 (2) 107–28

Reibstein, David J., and Paul W. Farris (1995), "Market Share and Distribution: A Generalization, a Speculation, and Some Implications." *Marketing Science* 14 (3) (Part 2 of 2), G190–202

Wilbur, Kenneth C., and Paul W. Farris (2006), "Using SKU-Level Share-Distribution Relationships as Distribution Forecast Aids for New CPG Products." Los Angeles, Calif.: University of Southern California, Working Paper

Internet Channels

The addition of an Internet channel to a firm's channel portfolio is evaluated positively, on average, by the stock market. This is partly due to the fact that this addition causes little or no inter-channel cannibalization.

Evidence base	80+ newspapers that added an Internet channel to their portfolio
Managerial implications	Managers should not unduly worry when deciding whether or not to add an Internet channel. Positive outcomes should not be taken for granted either, as the stock market reacts negatively in approximately 30% of all cases. Managers can influence the sign/size of this reaction by their entry timing and the extent of publicity given to the entry.
Contributor	Marnik G. Dekimpe, Tilburg University and Catholic University of Leuven
References	Deleersnyder, Barbara, Inge Geyskens, Katrijn Gielens, and Marnik G. Dekimpe (2002), "How Cannibalistic Is the Internet Channel? A Study of the Newspaper Industry in the United Kingdom and The Netherlands." *International Journal of Research in Marketing* 19 (4), 337–48
	Geyskens, Inge, Katrijn Gielens, and Marnik G. Dekimpe (2002), "The Market Valuation of Internet Channel Additions." *Journal of Marketing* 66 (2), 102–19

Out of Stock

The average retail out-of-stock incidence worldwide is 8.3%. The U.S. is at the low end (7.9%), Europe is at the high end (8.6%), and the rest of the world is 8.2%. More than half of out-of-stock situations last longer than 24 hours.

Evidence base	Summary of findings from 52 studies (16 published studies and 36 proprietary studies) of 32 fast-moving consumer goods categories from 71,000 customers from 29 countries
Managerial implications	A typical retailer loses about 4% of sales due to having items out of stock. This sales loss translates into an earnings per share loss of about $.012 (1.2 cents) for the average firm in the grocery retailing sector where the average earnings per share is about $.25 (25 cents) per year. Consumer response when faced with out of stock on store shelves range from buy at another store (31%), substitute another brand (26%), substitute same brand but different SKU (19%), delay purchase (15%), and do not purchase (9%). Seventy to seventy-five percent of out of stock is due to retailer practices including retailer ordering, forecasting, and shelving failures.
Contributors	Thomas Gruen, University of Colorado at Colorado Springs, Daniel Corsten, IE Business School, Madrid, and Sundar Bharadwaj, Emory University
Reference	Gruen, Thomas, Daniel Corsten, and Sundar Bharadwaj (2002), "Retail Out-of-Stocks: A Worldwide Examination of Extent, Causes, and Consumer Responses." Arlington, Va.: Food Marketing Institute and Grocery Manufacturers of America

14

Advertising

Overall Advertising Impact

The average sales-to-advertising elasticity is .1. It is higher for new products than established products, in Europe than the U.S., for durables than non-durables, and in print than TV. The advertising-to-sales elasticity is also lower in models that use disaggregate data and include advertising carryover, quality, or promotion.

Evidence base	Meta-analysis of over 262 brand level sales-to-advertising elasticities from over 130 separate brand-markets
Managerial implications	All else equal, relative advertising spending should be higher for newer than for older products, for durables relative to non-durables, and in print relative to TV. Great care should be taken in collecting disaggregate data and properly specifying the model for estimating advertising elasticity.
Contributor	Gerard J. Tellis, University of Southern California
References	Sethuraman, Raj, and Gerard J. Tellis (1991), "An Analysis of the Tradeoff Between Advertising and Pricing." *Journal of Marketing Research* 31 (2), 160–74
	Tellis, Gerard J. (2003), *Effective Advertising: How, When and Why Advertising Works.* Thousand Oaks, Calif.: Sage Publications

Long-term TV Advertising Impact

In cases where increased TV advertising has a significant impact on sales during the year of the weight increases, in the following two years, this sales impact is approximately doubled. On average, that doubling effect comes from an increase in buying rate in the test group. If TV advertising weight increases had no significant impact on sales during the first year, they had no impact in the two following years either.

Evidence base	55 TV advertising split cable tests which went on for three years where the only difference between test and control was the TV advertising treatment during the first year
Managerial implications	The impact of effective TV advertising is cumulative over at least a two-year period. However, if there is no significant effect in the short run, there is no significant effect in the long run. Thus, it is extremely profitable to find out whether TV advertising campaigns are working in the real world before putting big budgets behind them.
Contributor	Leonard M. Lodish, University of Pennsylvania
Reference	Lodish, Leonard, Magid M. Abraham, Jeanne Livelsberger, Beth Lubetkin, Bruce Richardson, and Mary Ellen Stevens (1995), "A Summary of Fifty-five In-Market Experimental Estimates of the Long-Term Effect of TV Advertising." *Marketing Science* 14 (3) (Part 2 of 2), G133–40

Determinants of Advertising Impact

Advertising impact depends on the product category. Specifically, advertising elasticities are as much as 50% higher for durables as for non-durables. In addition, advertising is more effective for experience than for search products.

Evidence base	Review of more than 200 studies on advertising
Managerial implications	Brands competing in product markets with high responsiveness to advertising should aggressively invest in advertising. Brands in markets with lower advertising effectiveness should carefully monitor their sales/advertising ratio and advertising ROI and invest more in other elements of the marketing mix.
Contributor	Demetrios Vakratsas, McGill University
References	Sethuraman, Raj, and Gerard J. Tellis (1991), "An Analysis of the Tradeoff Between Advertising and Price Discounting." *Journal of Marketing Research* 28 (2), 160–74
	Vakratsas, Demetrios, and Tim Ambler (1999), "How Advertising Works: What Do We Really Know?" *Journal of Marketing* 63 (1), 26–43

Advertising Impact and Competition

Higher competitive intensity (clutter) will result in lower advertising effectiveness. Competitive advertising may reduce elasticities by as much as 50%.

Evidence base	Multiple studies in packaged goods (e.g., personal care, detergents, ready-to-eat cereal) as well as durables (minivans, SUVs)
Managerial implications	Brands should overcome noise by advertising more heavily early on in the life cycle, when competitive intensity is lower, and "out-of-sync" with competitors, i.e., when their competitors do not advertise.
Contributor	Demetrios Vakratsas, McGill University
References	Danaher, Peter J., André Bonfrer, and Sanjay Dhar (2008), "The Effect of Competitive Advertising on Sales for Packaged Goods." *Journal of Marketing Research* 45 (2), 211–25
	Vakratsas, Demetrios, Fred M. Feinberg, Frank M. Bass, and Gurumurthy Kalyanaram (2004), "The Shape of Advertising Response Functions Revisited: A Model of Dynamic Probabilistic Thresholds." *Marketing Science* 23 (1), 109–19

Advertising Weight

The size and distribution of media weight is an important determinant of advertising effectiveness. The bigger the change in the media weight and the more concentrated it is, the greater the advertising effectiveness.

Evidence base	Meta-analysis of 389 TV advertising experiments and review of 50 media scheduling studies
Managerial implications	Brands should opt for heavily concentrated media plans with big bumps rather than evenly distributed or standard flighted plans.
Contributor	Demetrios Vakratsas, McGill University
References	Lodish, Leonard M., Magid Abraham, Stuart Kalmenson, Jeanne Livelsberger, Beth Lubetkin, Bruce Richardson, and Mary Ellen Stevens (1995), "How T.V. Advertising Works: A Meta-Analysis of 389 Real World Split Cable T.V. Experiments." *Journal of Marketing Research* 32 (2), 125–39

Vakratsas, Demetrios, and Prasad Naik (2007), "Essentials of Planning Media Schedules." In *Handbook of Advertising*, eds. Gerard J. Tellis and Tim Ambler, 333–48. Los Angeles, Calif.: Sage Publications |

Advertising Reference Price

The presence of an advertised reference in a price offer enhances consumers' internal reference price ($\eta = .26$) and their perceptions of value ($\eta = .21$) and lowers their intention to search for a lower price ($\eta = .17$). The level of the advertised reference in the price offer enhances consumers' internal reference price ($\eta = .29$) and their perceptions of value ($\eta = .25$) and lowers their intentions to search for a lower price ($\eta = .21$).

Evidence base	Meta-analysis of 38 studies
Managerial implications	As long as they adhere to "truth in advertising" and provide bona fide reference prices, managers should consider including them in the ads, promotions, and displays, as these reference prices are likely to convey appropriate levels of value and will motivate purchase intent. However, at the same time, public policy makers need to carefully monitor the use of advertised reference prices as they have a strong potential to deceive consumers if these advertised reference prices are not bona fide prices.
Contributors	Dhruv Grewal, Babson College, and Larry D. Compeau, Clarkson University
References	Compeau, Larry D., and Dhruv Grewal (1998), "Comparative Price Advertising: An Integrative Review." *Journal of Public Policy and Marketing* 17 (Fall), 257–74
	Grewal, Dhruv, and Larry D. Compeau (1992), "Comparative Price Advertising: Informative or Deceptive?" *Journal of Public Policy and Marketing* 11 (Spring), 52–62

Advertising Impact Duration

The average advertising duration interval on sales is brief—typically between six and nine months.

Evidence base	Aggregation-bias adjusted results from meta-analysis findings by Clarke (1976) across 70 studies and Assmus, Farley, and Lehmann (1984) across 128 models from 22 studies
Managerial implications	Managers should not expect that the tangible impact of their advertising lasts for years. In most cases it lasts less than three business quarters. Researchers should be aware of data aggregation bias, i.e., the longer the data interval (e.g., quarterly as compared to weekly), the longer the advertising effect appears to last.
Contributor	Robert P. Leone, Texas Christian University
References	Assmus, Gert, John U. Farley, and Donald R. Lehmann (1984), "How Advertising Affects Sales: Meta-Analysis of Econometric Results." *Journal of Marketing Research* 21 (1), 65–74 Bass, Frank M., and Robert P. Leone (1983) ,"Temporal Aggregation, the Data Interval Bias, and Empirical Estimation of Bimonthly Relations from Annual Data." *Management Science* 29 (1), 1–11 Clarke, D. G. (1976) "Econometric Measurement of the Duration of Advertising Effect on Sales." *Journal of Marketing Research* 13 (November), 345–57 Leone, Robert P. (1995), "Generalizing What Is Known About Temporal Aggregation and Advertising Carryover." *Marketing Science* 14 (3) (Part 2 of 2), G141–50

TV Advertising Effect

The average TV advertising to sales elasticity is .11 for established consumer products. It is higher for tests after 1995 than those before. There is a high variability in effects around these average elasticities. Some tests had elasticities over .5 and others were below −.05.

Evidence base	241 real-world TV advertising tests conducted by Information Resources, Inc. from 1989 to 2003
Managerial implications	To increase brand profits, it pays to test TV advertising in market prior to running it, thus only running TV campaigns that are generating returns higher than their costs.
Contributor	Leonard M. Lodish, University of Pennsylvania
References	Lodish, Leonard M., Magid Abraham, Stuart Kalmenson, Jeanne Livelsberger, Beth Lubetkin, Bruce Richardson, and Mary Ellen Stevens (1995), "How T.V. Advertising Works: A Meta-Analysis of 389 Real World Split Cable T.V. Experiments." *Journal of Marketing Research* 32 (2), 125–39
	Hu, Ye, Leonard M. Lodish, and Abba M. Krieger (2007), "An Analysis of Real World TV Advertising Tests: A 15-Year Update." *Journal of Advertising Research* 47 (3), 341–53

15

Marketing Mix

Household Response to Marketing

Sensitivity to marketing mix variables is predominantly a consumer trait and is not unique to specific product categories. In particular, higher-income households are less price sensitive and large families are more price sensitive. Households that visit the store often are more price sensitive. Households with larger market baskets are less price sensitive. Heavy-user households tend to be both less price sensitive and less display sensitive.

Evidence base	Consumer products: Bayesian multi-category model on panel data on five categories and 300 households
Managerial implications	Many firms offer multiple product categories. Given consumer types (bargain hunters, status conscious, etc.) that respond similarly across elements of the marketing mix, many aspects of such firms' marketing efforts can be common across the different product categories.
Contributor	Andrew Ainslie, UCLA
Reference	Ainslie, Andrew, and Peter E. Rossi (1998), "Similarities in Choice Behavior Across Product Categories." *Marketing Science* 17 (2), 91–106

Decomposition of Long-term Effects of Marketing Actions

Only 20% of the net sales effect of a marketing action is due to the initial campaign itself; most of the remaining effect stems from the synergy with other marketing actions (in the case of strategic actions such as new products and advertising) or from inertia (in the case of tactical actions such as price and feature).

Evidence base	Across 81 brands in 26 fast-moving consumer product categories
Managerial implications	Consumer reaction to the initial marketing action matters, but the net long-term effect is largely driven by company decisions to prolong the action and/or to support it with other marketing activities. Managers need to be aware of and attempt to capture such synergies in assessing the ROI of specific elements of (and the overall) marketing mix.
Contributor	Koen Pauwels, Ozyegin University and Dartmouth College
References	Pauwels, Koen (2004), "How Dynamic Consumer Response, Competitor Response, Company Support and Company Inertia Shape Long-Term Marketing Effectiveness." *Marketing Science* 23 (4), 596–610
	Pauwels, Koen (2007), "How Retailer and Competitor Decisions Drive the Long-Term Effectiveness of Manufacturer Promotions for Fast Moving Consumer Goods." *Journal of Retailing* 83 (3), 297–308

Mindset Metrics

Mindset metrics of awareness, consideration, and liking impact sales above and beyond the direct effect of advertising, price, distribution, and promotions on sales. Own and competitive mindset metrics account for about 16% of the variation in brand sales.

Evidence base	Analysis of over 74 brands in four categories over a seven-year period in France
Managerial implications	Building share in the customer's "mind and heart" translates into improved marketplace performance. Mindset metrics lead sales by several months, allowing time for managerial action before market performance itself is affected. When possible, mindset metrics should be included in sales response models.
Contributor	Shuba Srinivasan, Boston University
Reference	Srinivasan, Shuba, Marc Vanhuele, and Koen Pauwels (2008), "Do Mindset Metrics Explain Brand Sales?" Cambridge, Mass.: Marketing Science Institute, Report No. 08–119

Marketing/Sales Ratios

Marketing expenditures typically range between 10% and 20% of sales revenue. The ratios are highest for businesses with high gross profit margins. Sales force/sales ratios average three times advertising/sales ratios. Business-to-business (B-to-B) typically spend five to six times as much on sales force budgets as advertising, while spending only about half as much on total marketing as a percentage of sales as do business-to-consumer (B-to-C) businesses. Both B-to-B and B-to-C spend more on marketing/sales when selling new products, products purchased in low dollar amounts, and more frequently purchased products These generalizations are also consistent with meta-analyses of marginal elasticities for sales force and advertising spending.

Evidence base	Empirical studies of data from ADVISOR, PIMS, and COMPUSTAT
Managerial implications	These generalizations of marketing cost ratios provide broad benchmarks for spending, that is, what a firm "like yours" would most likely spend in a market like yours. These can be refined by experimental and econometric studies of response functions. Further, the generalizations can help project what changes in marketing spending are most likely to occur when market, competitive, or environmental conditions change.
Contributors	Paul Farris, University of Virginia, and Gary L. Lilien, Pennsylvania State University
References	Farris, Paul W., and Robert D. Buzzell (1979), "Why Advertising and Promotion Costs Vary: Some Cross Sectional Analyses." *Journal of Marketing* 43 (4), 112–22
	Lilien, Gary L. (1979), "ADVISOR 2: Modeling the Marketing Mix Decision for Industrial Products." *Management Science* 25 (2), 191–204

Lilien, Gary L., and David Weinstein (1984), "An International Comparison of the Determinants of Industrial Marketing Expenditures." *Journal of Marketing* 48 (1), 46–53

Reibstein, David J., Yogesh Joshi, and Paul W. Farris (2004), "Marketing Costs and Prices." In *The Profit Impact of Marketing Strategy Project: Retrospect and Prospects*, eds. Paul W. Farris and Michael J. Moore, 124–52. New York, N.Y.: Cambridge University Press

Post-launch Strategy and New-brand Performance

Among several elements of the marketing mix (pricing, discounting, feature and display, product-line length, distribution depth and breadth, and advertising), *distribution breadth* explains 54% of the observed variation in the market potential for new brands. The effects of the other elements are small relative to that of distribution.

Evidence base	Analysis of 225 new consumer brand launches in France
Managerial implications	As long as the *incremental* cost of obtaining additional distribution breadth (ACV) is less than 24% of retail sales, it is profitable to invest in distribution. The comparable figure for advertising is 1% of sales.
Contributor	Carl F. Mela, Duke University
Reference	Ataman, M. Berk, Carl F. Mela, and Harald J. van Heerde (2008), "Building Brands." *Marketing Science* 27 (6), 1036–54

16

Competitive Reaction

Competitive Reaction

The predominant form of competitive reaction to advertising and promotion attacks is to do nothing. For 54% of the brands under price-promotion attack, there is no short-run promotion reaction, and 85% of these brands do not react with advertising changes. By the same token, 82% of the brands under advertising attack do not react with advertising and 68% do not react with promotion. Long-run reactions happen even less often—occurring in less than 10% of the cases.

Evidence base	Analysis of reaction patterns for over 1,200 brands in 442 packaged goods categories covering four years of weekly scanner data in the Netherlands
Managerial implications	From a sales maximization point of view, most of the observed brands are justified in their decision not to react (88% of promotion cases and virtually all advertising instances). Managers should carefully consider alternatives before automatically responding in kind to competitors' promotions or advertising.
Contributors	Jan-Benedict E.M. Steenkamp, University of North Carolina at Chapel Hill, and Marnik G. Dekimpe, Tilburg University and Catholic University of Leuven
Reference	Steenkamp, Jan-Benedict E.M., Vincent R. Nijs, Dominique M. Hanssens, and Marnik G. Dekimpe (2005), "Competitive Reactions to Advertising and Promotion Attacks." *Marketing Science* 24 (1), 35–54

Concluding Comments

Replicable patterns in marketing exist and can often be quantified so that managers have access to benchmarks of marketing impact. I hope that this collection of generalizations has convinced the reader of this concluding statement. At the same time, we should realize that developing and testing these benchmarks is a work in progress, in particular in two important dimensions:

Some important areas of marketing have yet to accumulate enough knowledge for benchmarks to be formulated. In particular, two fields of practice come to mind: customer equity and Internet marketing. *Customer equity* is the sum of the lifetime values of a firm's customers. As such it provides an important connection between marketing strategy and long-term financial performance. I am grateful to V. Kumar of Georgia State University, who provided a collection of propositions from the business media on the components of customer equity—including customer acquisition, retention, cross-selling, and up-selling. However, these findings have yet to be scientifically tested before they could be considered empirical generalizations. Likewise, the area of *Internet marketing* is in need of generalizations, especially as related to the relative impact of traditional versus digital (interactive) media. While several important papers on Internet marketing have appeared, we need more replications before we can formulate new benchmarks. The current MSI research competition on "The Emergence and Impact of User-Generated Content" will be very helpful in this regard.

Several empirical generalizations need either sharper quantification, or replication in other sectors or regional markets, or additional contingencies. The reader will undoubtedly have noticed that some of the benchmarks in this volume are much more specific than others. In particular, generalizations on strategic topics tend to be less precise than those on tactical aspects of marketing. It is my hope that the gaps in our knowledge will serve as a catalyst for new research on marketing generalizations, for the benefit of marketing practitioners and marketing researchers alike.

ABOUT THE AUTHOR

Dominique M. Hanssens is the Bud Knapp Professor of Marketing at the UCLA Anderson Graduate School of Management, where he has been on the faculty since 1977. He has served as the school's faculty chair, associate dean, and marketing area chair. From 2005 to 2007 he served as Executive Director of the Marketing Science Institute in Cambridge, Massachusetts.

Hanssens studied econometrics at the University of Antwerp (B.S., 1974) in his native Belgium. He then pursued graduate study in marketing at Purdue University's Krannert Graduate School of Management, where he obtained an M.S. in 1976 and a Ph.D. in 1977. His research focuses on strategic marketing problems, in particular marketing productivity, to which he applies his expertise in data-analytic methods such as econometrics and time-series analysis. He serves or has served as an area editor for *Marketing Science* and an associate editor for *Management Science* and the *Journal of Marketing Research*. His papers have appeared in the leading academic and professional journals in marketing, economics, and statistics. Four of these articles have won Best Paper awards, in *Marketing Science* (1995, 2001, 2002) and *Journal of Marketing Research* (1999, 2007), and five were award finalists. The second edition of his book with Leonard Parsons and Randall Schultz, entitled *Market Response Models*, was published by Kluwer Academic Publishers in 2001 and translated into Chinese by Shanghai People's Publishing House in 2003. Hanssens won distinguished teaching awards in the UCLA MBA and Executive MBA programs and is a frequent contributor to the school's executive education offerings. In 2003 he was awarded the UCLA Anderson School's Neidorf "decade" teaching award, and in 2007 he was the recipient of the Churchill Lifetime Achievement Award of the American Marketing Association.

Hanssens' consulting experience covers strategic marketing problems such as allocating marketing resources, assessing long-term marketing effectiveness, and growing customer equity. His approach emphasizes market-response modeling on sophisticated customer and marketing databases. He has conducted assignments for Agilent Technologies, British Telecom, Mercedes, Disney, Google, Hewlett Packard, Hughes, Johnson & Johnson, Mattel Toys, Microsoft, Schwab, and Wells Fargo, among others. He is a partner with MarketShare Partners, a marketing analytics firm headquartered in Los Angeles.

ABOUT MSI

Founded in 1961, the Marketing Science Institute is a learning organization dedicated to bridging the gap between marketing science theory and business practice. MSI's worldwide network includes scholars from leading graduate schools of management and forward-looking managers from many of the world's most successful corporations.

As a nonprofit institution, MSI financially supports academic research for the development—and practical translation—of leading-edge marketing knowledge on topics of importance to business. Issues of key importance to business performance are identified by the Board of Trustees, which represents MSI corporations and the academic community. MSI supports studies by academics on these issues and disseminates the results through conferences and workshops, as well as through its publications series.